Dorothea Hamm

Von Apfel bis Zapfen

Apples, Cones & More

Kreative Weihnachtsfloristik von klein bis groß
Creative floral designs for Christmas in all sizes

Herausgeber *Publisher*	BLOOM's GmbH, Ratingen (D)
Konzeption *Concept*	Dorothea Hamm
Floristische Leitung *Direction Floral Art*	Klaus Wagener
Floristik *Floral Design*	Maike Bruder, Dany Eschenbüscher, Dorothea Hamm, Bettina von Hollen, Petra Klus, Stephan Pantze, Britta Peters
Redaktion *Editor*	Hella Henckel
Text *Text*	Carolin Fischer, Hella Henckel
Botanik *Botanicals*	Karl-Michael Haake
Übersetzung *Translation*	Fatiha El Mokrani
Grafische Gestaltung *Grafic Design*	Marion Hennig, Mandy Schubert
DTP *DTP*	Bettina Münch
Aufbau & Organisation *Organisation*	Alexander Hafke, Andreas Regalar
Herstellung *Production*	Print Partner, Bocholt (D)
Fotos *Photography*	Patrick Pantze-Werbefotografie GmbH, Lage (D)

© 2007 BLOOM's GmbH
Am Potekamp 6
D – 40885 Ratingen
Telefon: +49 2102 9644-0
Fax: +49 2102 896073
e-mail: info@blooms.de
www.blooms.de
1. Auflage 2007

ISBN 978-939868-84-2

Wir danken folgenden Personen und Firmen, in deren Räumen wir fotografieren durften:

Maike und Olaf Bruder, Oberkirchen
Firma Lohmeier Home Interiors, Bielefeld
Firma Möbel Heinrich GmbH, Bad Nenndorf
Möbelhaus Paul GmbH, Nienstädt
Melitta Beratungs- und Verwaltungs-GmbH Co KG, Minden

Dank auch an Firma Becker GmbH, Minden, die uns Produkte leihweise zur Verfügung stellte.

We thank the following persons and companies who provided us with their rooms for our photo shoots:

Maike and Olaf Bruder, Oberkirchen
Lohmeier Home Interiors, Bielefeld
Möbel Heinrich GmbH, Bad Nenndorf
Möbelhaus Paul GmbH, Nienstädt
Melitta Beratungs- und Verwaltungs-GmbH Co KG, Minden

We also thank the Becker GmbH in Minden who lent us their products.

Das Werk ist urheberrechtlich geschützt. Jede Verwertung ist ohne Zustimmung des Verlages oder des Herausgebers unzulässig und strafbar. Das gilt insbesondere für Vervielfältigungen, Übersetzungen, Mikroverfilmungen sowie die Einspeicherung und Verarbeitung in elektronischen Systemen.

This work is protected under copyright law. Any attempt to use the work without the consent of the publishing house or editor is inadmissible and punishable. This applies in particular to its duplication, translation, storage on microfilm and its storage and processing in electronic systems.

Inhalt/Content

Frucht   Apfel bis Mandel in Geschenkfloristik und Kerzenarrangements   6
Fruit   *Apples, almonds and more: floral gift designs and candle arrangements*

Zweig   Businessdekoration und Lichterarbeiten mit Zweigen   28
Branch   *Business decorations and Christmas lights with branches*

Pflanze   Christrose & Co: Ausgestaltungen für drinnen und draußen   70
Plant   *Helleborus and more: decorations for indoors and outdoors*

Zapfen   Holzige Naturformen in objekthaftem Raumschmuck   86
Cones   *Wooden forms combined with eye-catching room decorations*

| 112 | Laub- statt Nadelblätter im weihnachtlichen Flair | **Blatt** *Leaf* |

Foliage leaves instead of needles for the Christmas look

| 130 | Festlich aufgedeckt mit Protee, Eucharis oder Orchidee | **Blüte** *Flower* |

Festive table decorations with Protea, Eucharis and orchids

| 146 | Er darf nicht fehlen beim weihnachtlichen Fest | **Baum** *Tree* |

A must for every Christmas celebration!

| 154 | | **Service** *Service* |

Frucht
Fruit

Apfel, Nuss und Mandelkern gehören einfach in die Advents- und Weihnachtszeit. Früher galten sie als haltbare Nahrungsmittel und waren zur Festzeit Besonderheiten. Nüsse sind zudem Symbole des Lebens, der Apfel spiegelt im christlichen Sinne Schöpfung, Erbschuld und Erlösung wider. Kein Wunder also, dass sie auch wegen ihrer Farben für die floristischen Ideen auf den folgenden Seiten Pate standen. Vom klassischen Dunkelgrün-Rot bis hin zum modernen Mintgrün findet sich eine vielgestaltige Auswahl an kleinteiliger Geschenkfloristik, an Tischschmuckideen sowie lichterglänzendem Raumschmuck.

Apples, hazelnuts and almonds naturally belong to Advent and Christmas. In former times they were considered as durable food and were a specialty for the festive season. Furthermore, nuts symbolise life, and the apples reflect Creation, original sin and ransom according to the Christian belief. Thus, it is not astonishing that they were the inspiration for the floristic ideas presented on the following pages due to their colours. From classic dark-green-red to modern mint-green hues, this book contains a fabulous wealth of small floral gift ideas, tips for table decorations as well as shining room decorations.

Frucht *Fruit*

Vorweihnachtlich wird es, wenn zu Hause die Kerzen entzündet werden. Diese kleinen adventlichen Arrangements, deren zentraler Punkt ein rotbackiger Apfel ist, sind in der Kombination mit den grünen Kiefernnadeln farblich an das traditionelle Weihnachtsfest angelehnt. Einzeln, aber auch gruppiert aufgestellt, zieren sie manche Festtafel in der vorweihnachtlichen Zeit.

When the domestic candles are lighted, Christmas preparations are under way. These small Advent arrangements, emphasised by a red apple in the middle and combined with the green pine needles perfectly complement the traditional Christmas festival in terms of colours. As a solitary or grouped arrangement they decorate many a dinner table during the preliminary Christmas season.

Frucht *Fruit*

Hier haben glänzende Äpfel, die an rote, pausbackig strahlende Kindergesichter erinnern, ihren großen Auftritt. Auf dieser Seite sind sie dicht an dicht in einem Steckschaumwürfel befestigt und rücken die Kerzen so in ein rechtes Licht. Neben Sternen und anderen Symbolen ist auch die stilisierte Baumgestalt auf der linken Seite ein traditionelles Element in der Adventszeit. Gefertigt aus unterschiedlich großen Äpfeln verziert sie den Kerzenständer und verleiht ihm adventlich-festlichen Charme.

In this example, brilliant apples, which remind us of red, shining, chubby baby faces, are making their grand entrance. On the right, they are densely fixed within a floral foam cube, thus putting the candle in perspective. Besides the stars and other symbols, the stylised shape of the tree, shown on the left page, is also a traditional element of the Advent season. This construction made of differently sized apples decorates the candleholder with the festive charm of Advent.

Frucht *Fruit*

Ein Meer aus unterschiedlich großen Granatäpfeln bestimmt dieses Werkstück. Ihre verhärteten Kelchblattzipfel strecken sich dem Betrachter sternengleich entgegen. Um die Kerzen herum ziehen zudem leuchtende Beeren die Blicke auf sich. Durch den aufgelegten Kiefernzweig entsteht die Kombination der traditionellen weihnachtlichen Farben Rot und Grün.

A wealth of differently sized pomegranates is the focal point of this composition. Their hardened sepal points look like stars for the observers. Shining berries laid around the candles attract further attention. Thanks to the addition of a pine branch a combination of the traditional Christmas colours, red and green, is created.

Frucht *Fruit*

Diese kleinen Geschenkideen greifen das zur Weihnachtszeit typische Sternsymbol auf. Auch das den Granatapfel umkränzende Koniferengrün verbindet sich mit der weihnachtlichen Tradition. Die würzig duftenden Nelkenfrüchte galten zu Beginn der Zeitrechnung als Kostbarkeit und wurden als solche von den Heiligen Drei Königen bei ihrer Aufwartung dem Jesus-Kind als Geschenk mitgebracht.

These small gift ideas evoke the traditional symbol of the Christmas period, the star. The green conifers surrounding the pomegranate are associated with the traditional celebration of Christmas. The aromatic Carnation-fruits added to the composition were regarded as a treasure by the beginning of the Common Era and were brought as a gift to the baby Jesus by the three Wise Man.

Frucht *Fruit*

Seit jeher wird die rötlich-orange, Lampion ähnliche Frucht der *Physalis* als Winterschmuck benutzt. Hier wurden sie dicht an dicht nebeneinander auf einer runden Schale arrangiert. In dem Glanz der aufgelegten Christbaumkugel spiegeln sie sich reizvoll wider. Zusätzliche Dynamik bringt der aufgelegte, grün benadelte Zweig.

The red-orange Physalis-fruit, which looks like a lampion, has always been used as a winter decoration. Here, these fruits were densely and close to each other arranged within a round bowl. The brilliant Christmas ball reflects their charming beauty. The green conifer branch provides the composition with additional dynamism.

Frucht *Fruit*

Eine reizvolle Struktur entsteht durch aufeinander geschichtete Orangenscheiben. Darüber hinaus bereichert der angenehme Duft dieser Zitrusfrucht mit den aromatischen, ätherischen Ölen das adventliche Geschehen. Farblich dazu passend ist ein Wäldchen aus kleinen *Physalis*-Bäumchen, das prädestiniert ist, auf einem Tisch Aufstellung zu nehmen.

Layered orange slices create a beautiful texture. Furthermore, the pleasant scent of this citrus fruit with the essential oils enriches the Advent happening. A little forest composed of small Physalis-trees which suits the composition in terms of colour is designed to be presented on a table.

Frucht *Fruit*

Die klassischen Dauerfrüchte des Herbstes in der winterlichen Darstellung scheinen wie auf weiches Moos gebettet zu sein. Mittig und in einer Reihe hinzu gefügt, kontrastieren Sterne mit der rauen Oberfläche aus Rinde zum uniformen Auftritt der Walnüsse. Je nachdem in welcher Größe sie gearbeitet ist, eignet sich die Kugel durchaus als dekoratives Objekt für den Boden.

The classic permanent fruits of autumn look as if bedded on soft moss integrated into a wintry presentation. The raw textured stars made of bark which are also arranged in the middle and in the form of a row, contrast the uniform presentation of the walnuts. Depending on the respective size, the ball may absolutely lend itself as a decorative element for the ground.

Links zeichnen die Glück verheißenden Haselnüsse die Kontur des Baumes nach. Auch die Accessoires sind bewusst in warmen Brauntönen gehalten, um die Natürlichkeit des Werkstücks nicht zu verfremden. Highlight des rechten Baumes ist sein breiter Kragen aus verschiedenen Nüssen. Durch die unterschiedlichen Formen der eng nebeneinander aufgeklebten Wal-, Hasel-und Erdnüsse entsteht eine abwechslungsreiche Optik.

On the left, the hazelnuts symbolising luck, trace the outline of the tree. The selected accessories also show warm brown hues in order to keep the natural appearance of the composition. An eye-catching element of the tree on the right side is given by the wide sleeve composed of different nuts. Thanks to the different shape of the walnuts, hazelnuts and peanuts, which are glued next to each other, a diverse image is created.

Frucht *Fruit*

Es muss nicht immer klassisch sein, um festlich zu wirken. Die verwendeten, grünen Werkstoffe auf der mit Schlagmetall versilberten Holzplatte finden Halt zwischen Nägeln, die mit Draht umspannt sind. Auch die wie Stacheln nach oben stehenden Kiefernnadeln verleihen diesem ungewöhnlichen Adventskranz einen designten Charakter.

A design does not necessarily have to be classic in order to be classified as festive. The selected greeneries on the wooden plate silvered with metal leaf are held between nails, which are spanned by a wire. The vertical pine needles, which look like spines, provide this unusual Advent wreath with a unique look.

Frucht *Fruit*

Im Mittelmeerraum ist die Verwendung von Dattelpalmfrüchten zur Weihnachtszeit durchaus üblich. Links scheint die Kugel mit den abstehenden Kiefernnadeln sagen zu wollen: „Vorsicht! Stachelig!" Rechts wird die Stumpenkerze von einem üppigen Kragen umgeben, der ebenfalls aus den noch grünen Palmfrüchten mit ihren orangefarbenen Trieben gestaltet ist. Die Basis bilden grüne Holzstäbe.

The use of dates for Christmas is quite traditional in southern Europe. The ball on the left side entirely covered by the pine needles seems to caution against its spines. On the right side, the pillar candle is surrounded by a decorative sleeve, which is also composed of the green palm fruits at their orange shoots. The base is formed of green wooden sticks.

Zweig
Branch

Zweige – ob immergrün oder als Trockenmaterial – sind als Werkstoff aus der vorweihnachtlichen Floristik nicht wegzudenken. Begrünt in Form der winterfesten Nadeln sind sie das Symbol von Lebendigkeit und Lebenskraft der Natur in der ansonsten ruhenden Jahreszeit. Als entblätterte, kahle Zweige tragen sie das Erstarrte und Innehalten allen Wachstums im Winter zur Schau. Beides zusammen macht den Reiz bei den adventlich-weihnachtlichen Dekorationen aus. Lichterarbeiten, Business-Schmuck oder Adventskränze in verschiedenen Variationen mit stets dem gleichen Hauptdarsteller bringen festliche Stimmung ins Heim oder in die Firmenlobby.

Branches – whether in the form of evergreens or dry materials – are indispensable elements for the floral arrangements during the run-up to Christmas. Vegetated in the form of winter proofed needles they symbolise nature's vitality in this otherwise calm season. As defoliated, bare branches, they reveal the cold and lack winter. When combined they create the charm of Advent-Christmas decorations. Light decorations, business-accessories or Advent wreaths in different variations with the same main element provide homes or company offices with a festive atmosphere.

Zweig *Branch*

Ein Mistelzweig mit Früchten ist immer Glück verheißend. Und entsprechend reichlich werden immer mehr Mistelzweige zum Weihnachtsfest aufgehängt. Wie es der aus dem Angelsächsischen stammende Brauch will, wird unter diesem Adventskranz mit vier Kerzen und Mistelzweigen bestimmt der eine oder andere Kuss ausgetauscht.

Mistletoe with fruits always means luck. It is for this reason that mistletoes are increasingly and abundantly suspended at Christmas. According to this Anglo-Saxon custom, someone will definitely be kissed under this Advent wreath which consists of four candles and mistletoe.

Zweig Branch

Von der Decke herabhängende Mistelzweige sind an sich schon ein symbolischer Schmuck um die Weihnachtszeit. Schließlich tragen sie wie kaum ein anderer Zweig das im Winter rare Naturgrün in die Wohnräume. Je nach Art der Aufhängung und mit wenigen Accessoires akzentuiert, schmücken mal mehr die mit den weißlichen Beeren besetzten Triebe, mal die knorrigen, grünen Stängel des buschigen Schmarotzergewächses.

Misteloe hanging down the ceiling acts as a symbolic decoration for the time before and after Christmas. After all, unlike any other branch, they provide a living room with natural greeneries, which are so rare during winter. Depending on how they are suspended and emphasised with a few accessories, the decorations are either composed more by the shoots carrying the white berries or by the knotty green stems of this plant.

Zweig *Branch*

Das Brüchige, karg Winterliche unbelaubter Zweige stellt zu den edlen, weißblühenden Orchideen einen starken gestalterischen Kontrast dar. Damit wird das schmucke, mannshohe Arrangement zum festlichen Hingucker in einer Lobby oder einem großen Raum. Es braucht kaum noch der weihnachtlichen Schmuckaccessoires, lediglich ein paar kristalline Anhänger und versteckt ein paar Kugeln, um ihm die Daseinsberechtigung in der weihnachtlichen Zeit zu geben.

The uneven, meagre wintry image of defoliated branches is a stark contrast to the white noble orchids. As a result, the charming high arrangement becomes a festive eye-catching element within an entrance or vast room which does not require any further Christmas decorations. Only a few crystalline pendants and a few hidden Christmas balls are sufficient to underline the Christmas atmosphere.

Zweig Branch

Weihnachtlich und dennoch zurückhaltend modern präsentiert sich dieses Werkstück. Durch die Größe eignet es sich zum Beispiel für den Empfangs- und Eingangsbereich eines Firmengebäudes. Kreuz und quer eingesteckte Zweige holen ein Stück der erstarrten, verharrenden Natur in den Raum, die zu dem kubischen Sockel einen interessanten Gegensatz bildet. Glasschmuck, ein mit weicher, an frisch gefallenen Schnee erinnernder Watte beklebter Stern und die zarten, fragilen Trockenfrüchte schaffen festliche Bezüge auf ganz natürliche Art.

This composition is decorated with traditional yet discrete and modern Christmas accessories. Due to its size it lends itself as a decoration of the entrance of a company building. Branches which are irregularly inserted bring a piece of the frozen nature back into the room contrasting the cubic foot in an interesting manner. Glass decorations, a star pasted with cotton reminding us of fresh snow, as well as fragile dry fruits, create the festive atmosphere in a very natural manner.

Zweig Branch

Schlicht wirkt die Gefäßummantelung zu den cremefarbenen Blüten. Mit Flechte und Zapfen beklebt, scheint sie direkt aus der Natur entnommen. Repräsentativ dagegen ist der im kühlen Graublau gehaltene, stilisierte Baum. Durch Kugel- und Sternaccessoires bekommt die abstrakte Baumgestalt Bezug zum traditionellen Weihnachtsbaum.

In contrast to the cream blossoms, the coating of the container appears discrete. Pasted with lichen and cones it seems to be taken directly from nature. The stylised tree in cool grey-blue hues creates a symbolic image. Thanks to the ball and star accessories the abstract shape of the tree evokes a traditional Christmas tree.

Zweig *Branch*

Kerzenschein ist in der Adventszeit unverzichtbar. Er bringt Wärme und Gemütlichkeit gerade auch in Büroräume. Hier ragen die Kerzen aus der floralen Gestaltung heraus. So kann ihr Schein umso stärker erstrahlen, aber es geht auch keine Gefahr von den Flammen aus. Ihre Ständer sind von einem Gewirr aus knorrigen Obstbaumzweigen umgeben. In dem Miteinander von Ursprünglichkeit einerseits und festlichem Anspruch andererseits liegt die besondere Ausstrahlung dieses Raumschmucks.

Candle lights are indispensable for Advent, and thus provide even offices with a warm and cosy atmosphere. They may shine so much the stronger as the burning flames do not bear any risk. Their columns are surrounded by a tangle of knotty fruit tree branches. The contrast of tradition on the one hand and festivity on the other creates this unique room decoration.

Zweig *Branch*

Lichterarbeiten im wahrsten Sinne, auch wenn die Basis ganz ungewöhnlich aus den eher trostlos wirkenden Zweigen gestaltet wurde, aus denen jegliches Lebens entwichen zu sein scheint. Dafür setzen das strahlende Weiß der als rein geltenden Christrose und die glänzenden, dick bewachsten Äpfel Glanzpunkte in der Basis.

Indeed, in this example we have light decorations in the truest sense of the word, even if the base was very unusually constructed of rather desolate branches which seem to have lost any kind of life. In contrast, the shining white of the pure Helleborus and the brilliant abundantly waxed apples create the highlights of the base.

Zweig *Branch*

Blaue Akzente zur weihnachtlichen Zeit erinnern an die klirrende Kälte, die Eisblumen zum Erblühen bringt. Die frostige Anmutung kann durch das Bewachsen einzelner Äste unterstützt werden. Gespickt mit Accessoires in kühlem Blau, bringen diese filigranen Gestecke bezaubernde und winterliche Raffinesse in biedere Büroräume.

Blue accessories at Christmas call to mind the harsh cold which provokes the blossoming of the frost pattern. The frosty image may be underlined by waxing some of the branches. Decorating these filigree arrangements provides unsophisticated offices with a charming element of wintry refinement.

Zweig *Branch*

Beide Werkstücke arbeiten mit Accessoires in Blau, die einen modischen Akzent zu den bläulich wirkenden Nadelzweigen setzen. Der Stern steht sinnbildlich als Zeichen für besondere Ereignisse. Er leuchtete bei der Geburt Christi am nachtblauen Himmel, als Sternenkristalle finden sie sich überall in der winterlich-frostigen Welt.

Both compositions contain blue accessories, which create a modern accentuation for the bluish seeming pine needles. The star symbolises a particular event. It was shining in the blue night sky on the birth of Jesus; as star crystals they are found everywhere in the wintry-frosty world.

Zweig *Branch*

Durch ungewöhnliche Verarbeitung der Werkstoffe Aufmerksamkeit und Besonderheit zu erzeugen, ist die Kunst des Gestaltens. Bei diesem Kranz verursachen die entnadelten und wie Dornen nach außen stehenden unteren Triebenden der Nobilis-Tanne den Hingucker-Effekt. An den Spitzen eingesteckte blaue Schmucknadeln betonen zusätzlich.

The art of design is characterised by an unusual working of known or unusual materials and thus creating a focal point and something special. The needle-free and thorn-like shoot ends of the Nobilis-fir of this wreath determine the eye-catching effect. Blue decorative pins inserted at the points provide an additional accentuation.

Zweig *Branch*

Dieser schlicht gestaltete Kranz passt in reduziert eingerichtete, moderne Wohnungen. Glänzender Blickfang sind viele, verschieden große Christbaumkugeln, die die Kranzmitte schmücken. Die vier separat stehenden Stumpenkerzen markieren die vier Wochen und Sonntage bis zum Christfest. Eine adventliche Symbolik, die Johann Wiechern, ein protestantischer Pfarrer, Ende des vorletzten Jahrhunderts einführte, um seinen Zöglingen das Warten bis zum Weihnachtsfest zu veranschaulichen.

This discreetly designed wreath is suitable for simply furnished apartments. The various Christmas balls, which differ in size, decorate the middle of the wreath creating thus a brilliant highlight. The four separate pillar candles symbolise the four weeks and Sundays before Christmas; an Advent symbolism inaugurated by a Protestant priest, Johann Wiechern, at the end of the last century in order to demonstrate the waiting for Christmas to his pupil.

Zweig *Branch*

Häufig werden typische Weihnachtsfarben und auch Symbole schon in der Adventszeit verwendet. So verbinden die Menschen inzwischen mit einem dunklen Rot in Kombination mit klassischem Grün nicht nur das Weihnachtsfest, sondern bereits die vorweihnachtliche Zeit. Die beiden adventlichen Dekorationen sind in diesen Weihnachtsfarben gestaltet und werden durch silberne bzw. goldene Akzente noch veredelt.

In many cases, typical Christmas colours and also symbols are used for Advent. As a result, nowadays people do not only refer to Christmas in regard of dark red hues combined with classical green but also to the preceding period of Christmas preparations. Both Advent decorations are designed with Christmas colours and are further embellished by silvery or golden accentuations.

Zweig Branch

Man mag gar nicht vermuten, dass diese fantasievoll gearbeiteten Werkstücke einen einfachen Kerzenständer als Herzstück haben. Hier sind die Stumpenkerzen ganz und gar floristisch eingesetzt und ragen über den nach oben strebenden Ästen heraus. Besonders als Paar und in Reihe aufgestellt, machen sie durch ihre Höhe einen imposanten Eindruck.

It is hard to believe that these imaginative compositions contain a simple candleholder in the middle as their core. In this example, the pillar candles are completely used for floral purposes and tower above the ascending branches. They create an impressiv display due to their height, particularly if arranged as a couple and in the form of a row.

Zweig *Branch*

Für eine vorweihnachtliche Dekoration im modernen Firmengebäude ist die eigenwillige Kugelgestalt gedacht. Gestalterisch besticht das an der Decke hängende Objekt durch die in Ballierungsnetze kreuz und quer eingeflochtenen Ried- und *Cornus*-Zweige. Die darüber hinaus verarbeitete Stechpalme schützt sinnbildlich vor allem Bösen.

The individual shape of the ball is meant for the decoration of modern company buildings during the run-up to Christmas decorations. The creative aspect of the element hanging down the ceiling fascinates due to reed and Cornus branches irregularly interwoven into wire gauzes. The English holly used further symbolises protection against all evil.

Zweig *Branch*

Beide großteiligen Objekte sind gespickt mit weihnachtlichen Symbolen. Die abstrakte Baumgestalt links ist behängt mit Kugeln und die obere Platte gibt vielen Kerzen Platz. Äpfel, die Verbindung zum Paradies, und Zapfen, als Sinnbild für Fülle und Erfüllung, sind auf lange Metallstangen aufgespießt, durch die sich ein Kranz aus roten *Cornus*-Zweigen windet.

Both elements are decorated with Christmas symbols. The abstract tree form on the left is decorated with balls and the upper plate provides the surface for many candles. Finally, a burning candle symbolises Jesus's suffering according to the Christian belief. Apples, the reference to paradise and cones which symbolise wealth and fulfilment are speared onto long metal rods which are winded by a wreath made of Cornus branches.

Zweig *Branch*

Bei diesen Arrangements vermischt sich christliche und weltliche Symbolik. Abgestoßene Hörner als Fundstücke aus der Natur stellen sichtbare Zeichen eines natürlichen Prozesses dar. Symbole der winterlichen Natur sind unbelaubte Zweige, Früchte, immergrüne Koniferenzweige und Christrosen. Ganz verhalten leuchtet aus diesen Attributen der winterlichen Welt der Glanz des bevorstehendes Festes in Form der dunkelbraun glänzenden Kugeln hervor.

These arrangements present a mix of Christian and secular symbols. Broken horns as a discovery of nature represent a visible sign of a natural process as well as the candles. Defoliated branches, fruits, evergreen conifers and Helleborus are further symbols of the wintry nature. These elements of the wintry world very discretely evoke the shining of the upcoming festivity in the form of the dark brown shining balls.

Zweig *Branch*

Die auch in unseren Gefilden beheimatete Kiefer steht für Lebenskraft und Stärke, vor allem weil sie als immergrüne Konifere auch im Winter ihre grünen Nadeln trägt. Ihre ursprüngliche Baumgestalt ist hier gestalterisch nachempfunden worden in Form des Stehstraußes. Ein markanter Schmuck in der vorweihnachtlichen Zeit!

The pine which is also endemic to our regions symbolises life, energy and strength, particularly due to its green needles, which this evergreen conifer also shows in winter. Its original tree shape was decoratively imitated in the form of a traditional bouquet. A unique decoration for the period of the Christmas preparations!

Zweig *Branch*

Adventliche Dekorationen mit verspielten Akzenten bringen weihnachtliche Vorfreude für die ganze Familie. Der gestaltete Baum erinnert die Kinder Tag für Tag an den „richtigen" Weihnachtsbaum, unter dem am Heiligen Abend eifrig die Geschenke ausgepackt werden. Rechts beschützt ein Meer aus Kerzen die Engel, die aus der Kranzmitte zum Licht emporschauen.

Advent decorations with playful accentuations evoke the anticipation Christmas for the whole family. The designed tree reminds the children day by day of the "real" Christmas tree under which the presents are eagerly unwrapped on Christmas Eve. On the right page, a wealth of candles protects the angels, which look up to the light from the middle of the wreath.

Zweig *Branch*

Unverkennbar ist diese Lichterarbeit im Stil einer kindlichen Weihnacht gehalten. Dunkelrote Accessoires in Kombination mit Zapfen, die als spröde, braune Holzfrüchte gestalterisch ideal zu den rotwangigen Äpfeln passen, und die fröhlich-bunte Christbaumkugel drücken das familienorientierte, unkomplizierte und an Tradition orientierte Lebensgefühl aus.

This light decoration in the style of infantile Christmas is unmistakeable. Accessories in a dark red hue combined with cones, which perfectly suit the red apples in the form of rough brown wooden fruits, and the joyful Christmas ball expresses the family-friendly, uncomplicated and tradition-oriented attitude towards life.

Zweig *Branch*

Einfache Erstellung und eine hohe Wirkung ist hier sicher. Während links ein handelsübliches Zweiggerüst mit verschiedenen und für die Vorweihnachtszeit typischen Werkstoffen gefüllt ist, wurde das Gerüst auf der rechten Seite selbst gefertigt. Das rote Peddigrohr ist die beschützende Hülle für die *Cupressus*-Kugel.

An easy construction and a high effect are guaranteed for this example. While the usual branch framework on the left page is filled with materials which are typical of the pre-Christmas period, the framework on the left page is self-made. The red rattan core is the protective cover for the Cupressus-ball.

Pflanze
Plant

Wer an Pflanzen im Winter denkt, hat den Weihnachtsstern oder die Christrose vor Augen. Aber auch Orchideen und sogar Gräser lassen sich weihnachtlich gestalten. Heimelige Gemütlichkeit fürs Wohnzimmer oder festliche Dekoration für Terrasse und Balkon entstehen in Verbindung mit den traditionellen Weihnachtsfarben oder auch Symbolen. Verschiedene und von vornherein nicht unbedingt typische „Weihnachtspflanzen" verwandeln sich so zu den Vorboten des schönsten Festes am Ende des Jahres.

If one thinks of plants in winter, the Poinsettia *or the* Helleborus *are quickly called to mind. But orchids or even grasses can also be used for a Christmas decoration. A home-like cosiness for the living-room or a festive decoration for the terrace and balcony is created through the combination of traditional Christmas colours and symbols. Different and slightly untypical "Christmas plants" thus become the forerunners of the most beautiful festivity at the end of the year.*

Pflanze *Plant*

Eine Pflanze, die ihre Blüten trotz Kälte, Schnee und Eis öffnen kann, muss, so glaubte man, über magische Kräfte verfügen. Solch einer charismatischen Pflanze genügt somit eine schlichte Gestaltung. Hier erscheint sie als Topfpflanze mit wenigen Accessoires akzentuiert in ihrer vollen Pracht.

A plant, which opens its blossoms despite the cold, snow and ice, must, according to beliefs, dispose of magical energy. As a result, a simple design is sufficient for such a charismatic plant. In this example it is presented in its full splendour as a potted plant emphasised with a few accessories.

Pflanze *Plant*

Orchideen gelten als erlesen und wertig. Mit typisch weihnachtlichen Werkstoffen wie Zapfen und Kiefernnadeln kombiniert, werden auch sie zu Botschaftern, die die festliche Zeit einläuten. Ohnehin sind sie Präsente, die nahezu jeden Beschenkten erfreuen.

Orchids are regarded as select and valuable. Combined with typical Christmas elements, like cones and pine needles, they too become ambassadors who herald the festive season. Nevertheless, they are gifts, which make almost any person happy.

Pflanze *Plant*

Kaum einer weiß mehr, dass die Poinsettie nach ihrem Entdecker, dem amerikanischen Botschafter Joel Robert Poinsett benannt, eine aus Mexiko stammende, baumgroße Pflanze ist. So sehr prägt sie bereits seit Jahrzehnten aufgrund ihrer Blütezeit in den winterlichen Tagen unsere Weihnachtszeit. Und sie avancierte damit zum edlen Klassiker! Holzscheiben und Rinde in warmen Erdtönen umkleiden hier die Behältnisse, die die stolze Pflanze mit einer ihr gebührenden Ummantelung huldigen und durch ihre raue Struktur zu reizvollen Mitspielern werden.

Only a few people know that the Poinsettia, which was named after its discoverer, the American ambassador Robert Poinsett, is a tree-like plant originating from Mexico. For centuries it has characterised our Christmas period due to its blossoming time during winter when the days are short. And finally it thus became a noble classic! Wooden discs and bark in warm earthen hues cover these containers, which render homage to the proud plant through a worthy coating and through its raw texture classifying them as charming elements.

Pflanze *Plant*

Die Stieligkeit durch die blattlosen Schafte der prachtvollen Amaryllis wirkt bei diesen Ausarbeitungen mit und werden gestalterisch durch die Mikadostäbe nochmals aufgegriffen. Durch das satte „irdische" Rot der Blüte und den verarbeiteten Wollfäden wird der Bezug zum Advent hergestellt.

The stems of the leafless poles of this splendid Amaryllis influence their treatment within the composition and are creatively reflected by the use of Mikado sticks. With the help of the luscious "earthy" red hue of the blossom and the used woollen threads an image of Advent is created.

Pflanze *Plant*

Bei Fichte denken viele Menschen unmittelbar an den Weihnachtsbaum. Warum also dieses Image nicht gezielt bedienen und gestalterisch verstärken? Durch ihre Winterhärte eignet sie sich hervorragend, um Außenbereiche weihnachtlich zu schmücken. Mal als gebündelte Zweige, mal als ganzer Baum trotzt die Fichte nun hier dem Winter. Gespickt mit typischen Accessoires im weihnachtlichen Rot, mit Zapfen, Sternen und Bändern, verkündet sie auch auf Balkon oder Terrasse den Beginn der weihnachtlichen Zeit.

The fir is considered as the ultimate Christmas tree by many people. So, why not use this image and emphasise it creatively? Due to its stable condition in winter it lends itself perfectly as an outside decoration. Either in the form of bundled branches, or as a whole tree, the fir shows off in front of the wintry scenery. Decorated with the typical red Christmas accessories including cones, stars and ribbons, it announces the beginning of the Christmas period even on balcony or terraces.

Pflanze *Plant*

Der immergrüne Buchsbaum ist eine echte Alternative zu den im Winter beliebten Koniferen. Festlich mit Sternen oder übergestülpten Kränzen geschmückt, steht das immergrüne Gehölz mit dem dichten Blätterbesatz Fichte und Co. in nichts nach und macht auch vor der Haustür eine feierliche und dem Winter trotzende Figur.

The evergreen Box tree is a real alternative to the conifers, which are popular in winter. Owing to a festive decoration with stars and wreaths, the evergreen wood with its dense foliage is in no way inferior to the fir and the like. Furthermore, it embellishes a door entrance with a solemn welcoming by defying the winter at the same time.

Pflanze *Plant*

Modern und unkonventionell ist eine winterliche Außendekoration mit Gräsern. Trocken oder im saftigen Grün und in Kombination mit hellen Töpfen und Sternaccessoires stehen die Pflanzungen den Gästen beim Eintreffen zum Adventskaffee Spalier.

A winter decoration of the exterior with grasses is a modern and unconventional idea. The dry or fresh green planted arrangements combined with bright pots and star accessories welcome the guests to have a tea or coffee at Advent.

Zapfen
Cones

Zapfen sind Blütenstände, die aufgrund ihres Verholzens auch im Winter noch verfügbar sind und im dekorativen Bereich eingesetzt werden können. Als Symbol der Fülle und Erfüllung bestechen sie durch Vielgestaltigkeit und ihr attraktives, gleichmäßiges und wie von der Natur bewusst gestyltes Aussehen.

Cones are inflorescences which are also available in winter thanks to their wooden texture and can be used as a means of decoration. As the symbol of wealth and fulfilment they are inspiring, thanks to their complex shape and attractive, constant look which seems as if consciously designed by nature.

Zapfen *Cones*

Das Geheimnis dieses ausladenden Straußes ist sein Gerüst aus zusammen geschraubten Hölzern. Aufgeklebte Zapfen verleihen ihm in Kombination mit den transparenten „Amöben" und der modernen Lichterkette eine spannungsreiche Optik.

The secret of this voluminous bouquet is its framework of lumbers screwed together. Pasted cones provide this bouquet with an exciting look combined with the transparent "amoeba" and the modern Christmas lights.

Zapfen *Cones*

Traditionelle Werkstoffe führen nicht automatisch zu gewöhnlichen Werkstücken. Bestes Beispiel sind diese Lichterarbeiten. Sie reizen durch den farblichen Kontrast von hellem Holz und dunklen Zapfen. Zwischen Brettern oder Holzstäben finden viele von ihnen Halt und bestechen durch ihr sprödes und derbes Äußeres.

The use of traditional materials does not automatically generate ordinary compositions. The best example is given by the above-displayed light decorations. They are fascinating due to the contrasting colours of the bright wood and the dark cones. Many of them are held between boards or wooden sticks and are fascinating due to their rough and compact look.

Zapfen *Cones*

Hier kommt der verholzte Blütenstand der Koniferen zur vollen Geltung. Als Kissen, Stern oder Kranz. Diese Schmuckteile bringen einen winterlich-rauen Esprit in Wohnräume, was zur Zeit ganz aktuell ist.

In this example the wooden inflorescence of the conifers comes into one's own: in the form of a cushion, star or wreath. These decorative elements provide homes with a wintry cold atmosphere, thus underlining current trends.

Zapfen *Cones*

Scheiben aus Zapfen betonen flächige Dimensionen und verleihen adventlichen Schmuckformen eine neue Komponente. Bewusst sind Symbole integriert, die für Vollendung und Erfüllung stehen: Kreis und Symmetrie. So hat dieses Werkstück eine enge symbolische Verbindung zum Weihnachtsfest und greift über den Advent hinaus.

Discs made of cones underline laminar dimensions and adorn Advent decoration forms with a new element. Symbols which stand for perfection and completion were used with a certain intention: Circle and Symmetry. Thus, this composition is symbolically associated with the celebration of Christmas and goes beyond Advent.

Zapfen *Cones*

Es ist erstaunlich, welche Wirkung mit einer so bescheidenen Farbe wie Braun erzielt werden kann. Trockene Gräser, Blütenstände und verschiedene Zweige mal im Gerüst aus Draht, mal in einem aus Holzstäben eingeklemmt, passen gut in ein ländliches, naturverbundenes Ambiente und kommen ohne bunte Farbigkeit aus.

The effect realised with such a decent colour like brown is really amazing. Dry grasses, inflorescences and diverse twigs are put into a framework made of wire or of wooden sticks – where they are wedged in – are perfectly suitable for a rural, natural atmosphere, which does not require any other colours.

Zapfen *Cones*

Zapfen pur entfalten hier ihren ganzen Charme. Durch ihr reizvolles Äußeres benötigen sie keine zusätzlichen Accessoires. Mit Gefäßen und Unterlagen, die metallisch schimmern, entsteht eine modern angehauchte Waldhausromantik.

The pure charm of the cones is evoked in this example. Thanks to their beautiful look they do not require any additional accessories. With the help of containers and bases, which shimmer due to their metallic texture an atmosphere of a whiff of a modern romantic forest hut, is evoked.

Zapfen *Cones*

Der fünfzackige Stern steht für den Zusammenschluss von allen fünf weltbewegenden Elementen. Philosophen und Mystiker der Spätantike haben den bekannten vier Elementen – Feuer Erde, Wasser, Luft – ein fünftes hinzugefügt: das Licht. Der größte dieser vier Holzsterne ist durch aufgeklebte Zapfen zusätzlich hervorgehoben.

The five-pointed star stands for the combination of all five world-shaking elements. Philosophers and mystics of the Late Antiquity have added a fifth element to the four existing, fire, earth, water and air – the light. The biggest of these four wooden stars is additionally emphasised by glued cones stuck onto it.

Zapfen *Cones*

Die Zapfen des *Cupressus sempervirens* unterscheiden sich in ihrem Habitus deutlich von anderen Zapfen. Durch ihre kugelige Form eignen sie sich besonders für rundliche Dekorationen zum Advent. Bei den gezeigten Werkstücken werden sie kräftig durch goldene Akzente unterstützt. Gemeinhin steht Gold für etwas Vollendetes und gehört somit eigentlich in die Weihnachtszeit. Inzwischen jedoch schmücken Goldakzente bereits auch adventliche Dekorationen.

The texture of the Cupressus sempervirens-*cones clearly differs from other cones. Due to their spherical shape they lend themselves particularly well to round decorations for Advent. In the compositions shown here they are strongly supported by golden highlights. It is commonly accepted that gold symbolises perfection and thus belongs actually to the Christmas period. In the meanwhile, however, golden accentuations are also used for Advent decorations.*

Zapfen *Cones*

Ob als Gesteck-Manschette oder stilisierte Baumgestalt: *Cupressus*-Zapfen wie auch andere wirken insbesondere in gruppierter Anordnung. Vor allem, weil sich dann die spröden Holzformen zu einer reizvollen Oberfläche zusammentun, die damit neue und interessante Details aufweist.

Whether a florally arranged sleeve or stylised tree shapes: Cupressus-cones as well as other cones are particularly appealing if arranged in a group mainly because these combined rough wooden forms create a charming texture, which evokes new and interesting details.

Zapfen *Cones*

Im Advent spielen Äpfel und Zapfen ihre Reize am besten aus, wenn sie ohne Glanz und Glitter verarbeitet werden. Winterliches Beiwerk, wie hier die Kiefernnadeln, fügen sich dagegen harmonisch ein und bilden durch ihre Farbe einen klassischen Kontrast zum Rot der Äpfel.

The charm of apples and cones at Advent is at best presented if used without glamourous and glittering decorations. Wintry accessories, however, like the pine needles shown in this example, are included, harmoniously forming a classic contrast to the red apples due to their colour.

Zapfen *Cones*

Individuell und eigenwillig präsentieren sich diese Ausarbeitungen. Beim Gestalten mit Äpfeln und Zapfen ist gerade das Spiel mit den Größenverhältnissen reizvoll. Das linke Werkstück profitiert vor allem von verschiedenen Zapfenformen. Rechts bilden kleine Äpfel den Gegenpol zu den großen, angehängten Kiefernzapfen.

The design of these compositions appears individual and wilful. The combination of proportions is particularly interesting concerning designs with apples and cones. The composition shown on the left is mainly decorated by different cone forms. On the right, small apples contrast the big suspended pine cones.

Zapfen *Cones*

Hier besticht die Kombination aus braunen Zapfen und roten Accessoires. Die Kugel aus Bergkiefer-Zapfen thront auf einer Holzempore und wird von Zweigen bewacht. Rechts erhält die Manschette aus länglichen Zapfen eine fruchtige Füllung. Die roten Schmucksterne und die grünen Koniferenzweige greifen die typische Weihnachts-Farbigkeit auf.

This glamourous composition is constructed of brown cones combined with red accessories. The ball made of Pinus Mugo cones thrones above a wooden gallery and is adorned with twigs. On the right page, the sleeve of longish cones is filled with fruit materials. The red decorative stars and the green coniferous branches reflect the typical Christmas colours.

Blatt
Leaf

Blätter sind die typischen Träger des grünen Pflanzenfarbstoffs. Sie bringen die natürliche Vitalität in die Floristik. Gilt zwar das Koniferengrün, das der gerollten, nadelartigen Blätter, als das eigentliche Wintergrün, so können dennoch besondere Laubblätter hier eine interessante, gestalterische Alternative bieten.

Leaves typically carry the green plant pigment and provide floral designs with their natural vitality. Indeed, the green coniferous rolled, needle-like leaves are considered to symbolise the wintry green, however, particular foliage leaves may also serve as an interesting, creative alternative here.

Blatt *Leaf*

Auch der traditionelle Adventskranz kann modern gestaltet sein. Werden die weichen *Stachys*-Blätter dachziegelartig übereinander geschichtet, entsteht eine außergewöhnliche Optik. Der Schlichtheit dieses Kranzes wird durch die Gestaltung mit acht Kerzen wieder entsprochen.

Even the traditional Advent wreath can show a modern design. By layering the Stachys-*leaves in an imbricate arrangement onto each other an extraordinary image is created. The decency of the wreath is highlighted with the candle design.*

Blatt *Leaf*

Anspruchsvolles Floraldesign ist durchaus auch in der Adventszeit gefragt. Die mit *Stachys*-Blättern umhüllte Steckschaumkugel macht den Anschein, als ob *Eucalyptus* und *Lavandula* kraftvoll aus dem Innern der Kugel ausbrechen wollen. Bestärkt werden sie durch das helle Licht einer LED-Lichterkette.

Even during the Advent period sophisticated floral designs are absolutely demanded. The floral foam ball wrapped up with Stachys-leaves looks as if Eucalyptus and Lavandula want to break out of the interior of the ball. They are supported by the bright light of LED-lights.

Blatt *Leaf*

Kugeln sind Klassiker in der weihnachtlichen Zeit. Von ihrer Form her symbolisieren sie Vollkommenheit. Mal mit Scherben von einer Christbaumkugel beklebt, mal mit Holzscheiben oder Anisfrüchten – gruppiert angeordnet machen sie aus jedem Tisch eine Festtafel.

Spheres are a classic element at Christmas time. Their form symbolises perfection. Whether adorned with broken fragments of a Christmas ball or with wooden discs or anise fruits – in a grouped arrangement they make every table a fabulous dinner table.

Blatt *Leaf*

Grün steht für das Leben und für die Hoffnung. Wer kennt nicht die bekannte Weihnachtslied-Strophe: „Oh Tannenbaum, wie grün sind deine Blätter" – auch wenn es sich um Nadeln handelt. So können hier die wintergrünen *Eucalyptus*-Blätter als Hoffnung auf ein baldiges Wiederaufleben der Natur interpretiert werden.

Green symbolises life and also hope. There is a famous Christmas carol of German origin "Oh Christmas tree! How are thy leaves so verdant!" – reflecting this image even if a fir tree carries needles. Thus, the wintry green Eucalyptus-leaves can be interpreted as the hope for nature's swift revival.

Blatt *Leaf*

Hinter dem immergrünen Efeu steht der Gedanke der Unsterblichkeit. Außergewöhnlich bei diesem Kranz: Die *Hedera*-Blätter sind umgekehrt angebracht, so dass die Blattstiele in alle Richtungen herausschauen. Wiederum klassisch ist die Kombination mit roten Stumpenkerzen, deren Halter durch Schnecken aus Filzband verdeckt sind.

The evergreen ivy stands for immortality. An extraordinary aspect of this wreath: The Hedera-leaves are arranged upside down so that the petioles stick out in all directions. A classic element is the combination of red pillar candles, whose sticks are covered with felt ribbon wrapped around in a spiral.

Blatt *Leaf*

Das Geheimnis dieser gezackten und mit *Hedera* beklebten Manschette ist einfache Tonpappe. Sie verhilft den in Steckschaum eingesteckten Werkstoffen und dem Pompon zu einem großen Auftritt. Diese Gestecke beweisen es: Als klassisches Paar in der Weihnachtszeit sind Rot und Grün unschlagbar.

The secret of this jagged sleeve, which is pasted with Hedera, is the use of simple cardboard. It helps create a wonderful image with the materials inserted into the floral foam and the pompon. These arrangements are the best example: The classic combination of red and green is unbeatable.

Blatt *Leaf*

Die sattgrünen Blätter der Stechpalme und dazu die roten Beeren erscheinen in der dunkelsten Jahreszeit als glücksbringende Symbole. Schließlich sind diese Farben die Farben der Hoffnung und der Liebe. Bei den adventlichen Dekorationen steht der rote Apfel stellvertretend für die Beeren.

The fresh green leaves of the English holly complemented with the red berries symbolise luck during the darkest season of the year. And last but not least these colours stand for hope and love. The red apple of the Advent decorations represents the berries.

Blatt *Leaf*

Auch eine einzelne Kerze verbreitet Vorfreude auf das Weihnachtsfest. Außergewöhnlich ist eine mit *Ilex*-Blättern beklebte Schale als Untersetzer. Die aufgelegten Zapfen und Äste bringen darüber hinaus ein Stück Waldromantik ins festlich geschmückte Heim.

Even a single candle evokes Christmas anticipations. A bowl pasted with Ilex-leaves in the form of a trivet. Furthermore, the cones and branches laid upon it evoke an atmosphere of forest romance within the festively decorated home.

Blüte
Blossom

Nur wenige Blüten verbinden sich traditionell mit der weihnachtlichen Festsymbolik. Hierzu gehören die raren Winterblüher wie die Christrose, eine in Mitteleuropa eingebürgerte Pflanze, sowie einige Zwiebelblüher. Auf der anderen Seite sind es die Zugereisten, deren Blütezeit am Heimatstandort in unserem Winter liegt. Die edlen Orchideen zählen hierzu. Alle zusammen repräsentieren sie weihnachtliche Festlichkeit.

Only a few blossoms are associated with the traditional celebration of Christmas, including the rare winter blossoms, such as Helleborus, a plant native to Central Europe, as well as some flower bulbs. On the other hand, imported flowers, such as the noble orchids, are blooming in their native countries during our winters. Altogether they create a traditional and festive Christmas atmosphere.

Blüte *Blossom*

Das perfekte Zusammenspiel von Geschirr, Gläsern und Floristik ist für eine gelungene Festtafel von großer Bedeutung. Vom Kerzenständer bis hin zur Serviettengestaltung sollte alles stimmig sein. An die Kerzenleuchter sind weiß gestrichene *Betula*-Zweige angebracht, die den Werkstoffen als haltgebendes Gerüst dienen.

The perfect combination of dishes, glasses and floral designs is of immense importance for a successful dinner table. From the candlestick to the napkin decoration, the image should be harmonious. The candlesticks are adorned with Betula-twigs painted in white which serve as a framework for the materials.

Blüte *Blossom*

Bei der Serviettendekoration wie auch den kleinen floralen Arrangements ist *Helleborus* das wiederkehrende Gestaltungselement. Außerdem immer mit dabei: Die weiß gestrichenen *Betula*-Zweige. Alles in allem steht bei dieser Tischdekoration einer „weißen Weihnacht" nichts mehr im Wege.

Helleborus is a recurring element used for the design of the napkin decoration and the small floral arrangements. Furthermore, the Betula-twigs are always used. With this table decoration the dream of a "white Christmas" may come true.

Blüte *Blossom*

Die *Eucharis*, auch Stern von Bethlehem genannt, passt nicht nur aufgrund ihres Namens in die weihnachtliche Zeit. Ihre weißen, fast sternenförmigen Blüten blühen auch in der kalten Jahreszeit und verschönern so adventliche Dekorationen durch ihr majestätisches Antlitz. Ihre langen Stiele kommen in hohen, schlanken Gefäßen gut zur Geltung.

The Eucharis, also called Star of Bethlehem, is not only suitable for Christmas due to its name. Its white almost star-like blossoms also flourish during this cold season and thus embellish Advent decorations thanks to their majestic countenance. Its long stems are best presented in high, slim containers.

Blüte *Blossom*

Das Beste ist gerade gut genug. Nach diesem Motto sind diese Arrangements mit der *Protea* gestaltet. Durch die weihnachtlichen Accessoires und Werkstoffe wie Zapfen oder Granatapfel werden diese Werkstücke zu adventlichen Dekorationen für die anspruchsvolle Kundschaft.

Only the best is good enough. This is exactly what these arrangements evoke, being decorated with the Protea. Thanks to the Christmas accessories and materials like cones or pomegranates these compositions become Advent decorations for sophisticated customers.

Blüte *Blossom*

Dieses Ambiente eignet sich perfekt für ein festliches Essen am Heiligen Abend, denn das Zusammenspiel von dem Braun der Zapfen und den rötlichen Blüten wirkt besonders edel. Durch zusätzliche liebevoll gestaltete Details wie Namensschilder wird der Tisch zu einer wahren Prachttafel.

This atmosphere is perfectly suitable for a festive dinner at Christmas Eve due to the combination of the brown cones and the reddish blossoms which appear particularly noble. Thanks to the lovely decorated details like name plates, the table becomes a really magnificent element.

Blüte *Blossom*

Die interessant gemusterte Blüte der *Phalaenopsis* ist der Blickfang bei der Serviettendekoration und dem Wandbild. Das Namensschild besticht durch die Schichtung der unterschiedlichen Werkstoffe, deren Krönung ein Granatapfel ist. Platz für den Namen bietet dabei eine einfache Holzkugel.

The Phalaenopsis-*blossom with its interesting pattern is the eye-catching element of the napkin decoration and the mural. The name plate is fascinating due to the layering of the different materials which are highlighted with a pomegranate. The name is written on a simple wooden sphere.*

Blüte *Blossom*

Die Amaryllis in ihrem klassischen Rot ist prädestiniert für adventliche Ausgestaltungen. Durch ihre Stiellänge wirken sie auch in breiten oder hohen Gefäßen. Links findet sie durch ein Zweiggerüst gesteckt Halt, rechts ist sie mit Zimtrinde kombiniert. Der Duft dieses Gewürzes weckt seit jeher weihnachtliche Gefühle.

The Amaryllis in its classic red is perfect for Advent decorations. Due to their long petioles they are also effectively presented in large and high containers. On the left, it is supported by a branch framework into which it is inserted and on the right it is combined with cinnamon bark. The scent of this spice has always evoked Christmas feelings.

Baum
Tree

Kein anderer Baum repräsentiert das winterliche Fest so wie der poetisch bezeichnete „Tannenbaum", womit im botanischen Sinne die Fichte gemeint ist. Doch auch andere Koniferen, die über ein winterliches, immergrünes Nadelkleid verfügen, wie Kiefer oder sogar die blaugrüne Zeder, bieten reizvolle Alternativen für den grünen Hoffnungsträger in der unwirtlichen, wachstumsarmen Winterzeit.

No other tree symbolises the celebration of Christmas like the Christmas tree or Tannenbaum (German for fir tree). However, other evergreen coniferous trees, such as the pine or the blue green cedar provides a charming alternative for the green bearer of hope in this unsociable winter time of poor growth.

Baum *Tree*

Die hier verwendete Kiefer steht sinnbildlich für Lebenskraft. Echte Kerzen ersetzen die elektrische Lichterkette und verbreiten mit ihrem Schein heimelige Gemütlichkeit. Bei der weiteren Ausgestaltung ist Natürlichkeit Trumpf. Die eingehängten Sterne sind überwiegend aus Naturmaterialien wie Zimt, Rinde oder Stroh.

The pine used for this composition symbolises vitality. Real candles are used instead of the electric Christmas lights and evoke an atmosphere of homey cosiness through their flames. The further decoration is highlighted with natural elements. The suspended stars mainly consist of natural elements like cinnamon, bark or straw.

Baum *Tree*

Unkonventionell und doch traditionell mutet dieser Weihnachtsbaum an. Bekannt sind die nordisch angehauchten Accessoires. Ausgefallen dagegen ist es, den unteren Bereich des Stammes von den Ästen zu befreien. So wird die Aufmerksamkeit auf die an langen Bändern befestigten Holzscheiben, Zapfen und Süßigkeiten gelenkt.

This Christmas tree appears unconventional yet traditional. The apparently Nordic accessories are recurring Christmas elements. In contrast to that, it is rather unusual to remove the branches of the lower part of a stem. Thus, people's attention is drawn to the wooden discs, cones and sweets fixed onto long ribbons.

Baum *Tree*

Zedern stehen im übertragenen Sinne für die christliche Kirche. Beweis dafür ist ihre häufige Erwähnung in der Bibel. Durch den transparenten und helltonigen Schmuck strahlt dieser Weihnachtsbaum moderne Eleganz aus. Raffiniert: Die farblich passenden und frischen *Helleborus* sind in Glasröhrchen in den Baum gehängt.

Cedars symbolise the Christian church in the figurative sense. This is evidenced by several references to it in the bible. Thanks to the transparent and bright decoration this Christmas tree evokes a modern elegant image. As a refining element, the appropriate fresh Helleborus *put into glass tubes are suspended at the tree.*

Service/Service

Frucht/*Fruit*

Seite 8/9:
Werkstoffe: *Malus Cultivar, Pinus mugo*
Materialien: Tontopf, Filzband, Blei, Kerze
Wie wird's gemacht: Der umgedrehte Tontopf ist rundherum mit parallel gefassten Kiefernnadeln umklebt, die zusätzlich mit einem Filzband umwickelt werden. Die Kerze wird angedrahtet, mit einem Streifen Blei umwickelt und in den Apfel gesteckt.
Page 8/9:
Botanicals: *Malus Cultivar, Pinus mugo*
Non-floral materials: *Clay pot, felt ribbon, lead, candle*
How to make it: *The upside down clay pot is pasted all over with parallel formed pine needles which are then wrapped up with a felt ribbon. The candle is wired, entwined with a stripe of lead and put into the apple.*

Seite 10:
Werkstoffe: *Malus Cultivars*
Materialien: Gipsfuß mit Stange und Kerzenhalter, Draht, Blei, Kerze
Wie wird's gemacht: Für dieses Kerzenarrangement wird ein handelsüblicher Ständer mit abgespultem Draht und darin eingeklemmten Äpfeln versehen. Der Gipsfuß erhält eine Bleiumwicklung.
Page 10:
Botanicals: *Malus Cultivars*
Non-floral materials: *Gypsum foot with bar and candleholder, wire, lead, candle*
How to make it: *For this candle arrangement, a usual rod is provided with an uncoiled wire and apples wedged into. The gypsum foot is wrapped up with lead.*

Seite 11:
Werkstoffe: *Malus Cultivar,* Moos
Materialien: Steckschaumwürfel, Kerzen, Zahnstocher, Blei
Wie wird's gemacht: Die Äpfel werden mit Hilfe von Zahnstochern auf den mit Moos umwickelten Steckschaumwürfel gesteckt, ebenso die angedrahteten und im unteren Bereich mit einem Streifen aus Blei umwickelten Kerzen. Ein Bleistern bildet den zusätzlichen Schmuckakzent.
Page 11:
Botanicals: *Malus Cultivar, moss*
Non-floral materials: *Floral foam cube, candles, tooth picks, lead*
How to make it: *The apples are inserted into the floral foam cube wrapped up with moss with the help of tooth picks as well as the wired candies, which are decorated with lead stripes at their lower part. A leaded star further decorates the construction.*

Seite 12/13:
Werkstoffe: *Malus Cultivars, Pinus nigra, Punica granatum, Vaccinium macrocarpon*
Materialien: Steckschaum, Schale, Kerzen
Wie wird's gemacht: Die Schale wird mit Steckschaum ausgelegt und mit angedrahteten *Punica granatum*-Früchten besteckt. Um die Kerzen die anderen Früchte streuen, den Kiefernzweig auflegen und die vier Kerzen einstecken.
Page 12/13:
Botanicals: *Malus Cultivars, Pinus nigra, Punica granatum, Vaccinium macrocarpon*
Non-floral materials: *Floral foam, bowl, candles*
How to make it: *The bowl is filled with floral foam and decorated with wired Punica granatum-fruits. Spread the other fruits around the candles, put on the pine wreath and insert the four candles.*

Seite 14:
Werkstoffe: *Juniperus squamata, Punica granatum,* Gewürznelken
Materialien: Topf, Draht, Dekostern
Wie wird's gemacht: Schalen mit Steckschaum füllen und je einen Granatapfel auflegen. Diese mit einem gewickelten Kranz aus Wacholder umlegen. Die Nelkenfrüchte werden zur Akzentuierung aufgeklebt und der Dekostern angebracht.
Page 14:
Botanicals: *Juniperus squamata, Punica granatum, cloves*
Non-floral materials: *Pot, wire, decorative star*
How to make it: *Fill the bowls with floral foam and put one pomegranate on top. Lay a wreath wrapped up in juniper around these containers. The carnation fruits are stuck and the decorative star attached to the composition.*

Seite 15:
Werkstoffe: *Juniperus squamata, Punica granatum, Proboscidea louisianica,* Baumschwämme
Materialien: Lichterkette, Dekosterne, Splittstäbe, Draht, Vase
Wie wird's gemacht: Für die Manschette werden die handelsüblichen Sterne übereinander geschichtet und eine Lichterkette dazwischen gelegt. Die Trockenmaterialien sind angedrahtet und die Früchte auf Holzstäbe gespießt. So können die Werkstoffe nun zu einem Strauß gebunden werden, der durch die Stern-Manschette in die Vase gestellt wird.
Page 15:
Botanicals: *Juniperus squamata, Punica granatum, Proboscidea louisianica, bracket fungi*
Non-floral materials: *Christmas lights, decorative stars, split sticks, wire, vase*
How to make it: *To create a sleeve the usual stars are layered and a string of Christmas lights is put in-between. The dry materials are wired and the fruits are spiked on wooden sticks. Thus, the materials can be tied together in the form of a bouquet, which is inserted through the star sleeve into the vase.*

Seite 16/17:
Werkstoffe: *Chamaecyparis pisifera, Physalis alkekengi*
Materialien: Schale, Kugel
Wie wird's gemacht: Die *Physalis*-Früchte sind mit Heißkleber auf die Schale geklebt. Als Hingucker eine Dekokugel in die Mitte legen und zusätzlich *Chamaecyparis*-Zweig arrangieren.
Page 16/17:
Botanicals: *Chamaecyparis pisifera, Physalis alkekengi*
Non-floral materials: *Bowl, ball*
How to make it: *The Physalis-fruits are pasted onto the bowl with hot glue. Put a decorative ball into the middle as an eye-catching ornament and decorate further with a Chamaecyparis-twig.*

Seite 18:
Werkstoffe: *Physalis alkekengi,* Kiefernnadeln
Materialien: Metallbäumchen, Vasen, Draht
Wie wird's gemacht: Das Metallbäumchen mit *Physalis*-Früchten füllen und zusätzlich mit Draht umwickeln, damit sie nicht herausfallen. Die Kiefernnadeln rundherum in die Baumform stecken.
Page 18:
Botanicals: *Physalis alkekengi, pine needles*
Non-floral materials: *Small metal tree, vases, wire*
How to make it: *Fill the metal tree with Physalis-fruits and wrap them with wire to prevent them from falling out. Insert the pine needles all around the tree.*

Seite 19:
Werkstoffe: *Cryptomeria japonica, Physalis alkekengi,* Orangenscheiben
Materialien: Band, Gefäß, Kerze
Wie wird's gemacht: Schichtweise werden die Orangenschalen auf das Gefäß geklebt. Für die hängende Dekoration werden jeweils eine *Physalis*, eine Orangenscheibe und ein Filzstern auf Band gefädelt, und dieses anschließend an den Orangenscheiben befestigt.
Page 19:
Botanicals: *Cryptomeria japonica, Physalis alkekengi, orange slices*
Non-floral materials: *Ribbon, container, candle*
How to make it: *The oranges slices are stuck in layers onto the container. The suspended decoration is respectively constructed of a Physalis-fruit, combined with an orange slice and a felt star which are threaded onto a ribbon which is finally attached onto the orange slices.*

Seite 20/21:
Werkstoffe: Moos, Walnüsse
Materialien: Styroporkugel, Birkenrindensterne, Draht
Wie wird's gemacht: Die Styroporkugel dicht mit Moos bekleben. Anschließend die Walnüsse mit leichtem Abstand zueinander aufkleben. Die angedrahteten Sterne im Bereich des „Äquators" nebeneinander in die Kugel stecken.
Page 20/21:
Botanicals: *Moss, walnuts*
Non-floral materials: *Styrofoam-ball, stars of birchbark, wire*
How to make it: *Paste the Styrofoam-ball in a dense arrangement with moss. Then, adhere the walnuts with a slight distance to each other on top. insert the wired stars in a parallel form in the equatorial area of the ball.*

Seite 22:
Werkstoffe: Haselnüsse, Bäume aus Rinde
Materialien: Dekosterne
Wie wird's gemacht: Die Haselnüsse wie eine Umrisslinie seitlich auf den handelsüblichen Baum aus Rinde aufkleben. Als Akzente werden die Metallsterne mit kleinen Nägeln an dem Baum befestigt.
Page 22:
Botanicals: *Hazelnuts, bark trees*
Non-floral materials: *Decorative stones*
How to make it: *Stick the hazelnuts alongside the usual tree made of bark. The metal stars serve as an additional decoration and are fixed onto the tree with the help of little nails.*

Seite 23:
Werkstoffe: Moos, Walnüsse, Haselnüsse, Erdnüsse, Baumstamm, Holzstab
Materialien: Steckschaumkegel, Wickeldraht, Steckdraht, Dekostern
Wie wird's gemacht: Für die Baumgestalt wird ein Steckschaumkegel mit Moos bewickelt. Auf den unteren Kegelmantel einen Rand aus Nüssen kleben. Die Spitze wird mit silbernem Draht umwickelt und einem angedrahteten Stern akzentuiert. Zum Schluss wird der Kegel mit einem Ast auf einem Holzstamm befestigt.
Page 23:
Botanicals: *Moss, walnuts, hazelnuts, peanuts, bole, wooden stick*
Non-floral materials: *Floral foam cone, binding wire, florist wire, decorative star*
How to make it: *A floral foam cone is wrapped up with moss to create the tree construction. Stick a frame of nuts onto the lower part of the cone. The point is wrapped with a silvery wire and emphasised with a wired star. At the end, the cone is attached to a bole with a branch.*

Seite 24/25:
Werkstoffe: *Chamaerops humilis, Pinus nigra, Sempervivum x fauconnettii*
Materialien: Brett, Schlagmetall, Blei, Kerzen, Zierdraht, Nagel
Wie wird's gemacht: Eine quadratische Holzplatte wird mit Schlagmetall versilbert. Als „Kranzgerüst" dienen kreisförmig eingeschlagene Nägel, die mit Draht umspannt werden. Die Palmenfrüchte werden eingeklemmt und *Sempervivum*-Rosetten dazwischen gesetzt. Zusätzlich einige Zapfen einklemmen und Kiefernnadeln mit Sprühkleber im Kranz befestigen. Die Kerzen auf eingeschlagene Metallstifte setzen und unten mit Blei umkleiden.
Page 24/25:
Botanicals: *Chamaerops humilis, Pinus nigra, Sempervivum x fauconnettii*
Non-floral materials: *Board, metal leaf, lead, candles, decorative wire, nail*
How to make it: *A square wooden plate is silvered with metal leaf. The framework of this wreath is constructed of nails which are spanned by a wire and circularly driven into the board. The palm fruits are wedged in and Sempervivum-rosettes are put in-between. In addition, a few cones are wedged in and pine needles are attached to the wreath with adhesive spray. Put the candles into the metal aglets driven into the board and cover with lead at the bottom.*

Seite 26:
Werkstoffe: *Chamaerops humilis, Pinus nigra*
Materialien: Drahtkugel, Draht, Kerzenhalter, Kerzen
Wie wird's gemacht: Die Früchte der *Chamaerops* werden mit Haften in die handelsübliche Drahtkugel gesteckt und die Kiefernnadeln mit Sprühkleber befestigt. Zum Schluss die Kerzenhalter in die Kugel kleben und die Kerzen einsetzen.
Page 26:
Botanicals: *Chamaerops humilis, Pinus nigra*
Non-floral materials: *Wired ball, wire, candleholder, candles*
How to make it: *The fruits of the Chamaerops are inserted into the usual wire ball with the help of clamps and the pine needles are fixed with adhesive spray. At the end, stick the candleholders into the ball and insert the candles.*

Seite 27:
Werkstoffe: *Chamaerops humilis, Pinus nigra,* Holzstäbe
Materialien: Kerzenständer, Schlagmetall, Baumschulnetz, Dekosterne, Kerze
Wie wird's gemacht: Für die Manschette werden mehrere grüne Holzstäbe zur Stabilisierung kreuz und quer in ein Baumschulnetz eingeflochten und dann die Früchte der *Chamaerops* mit Draht darauf befestigt. Zusätzlich die Kiefernnadeln mit Sprühkleber fixieren und die versilberten Sterne auf die Manschette kleben.
Page 27:
Botanicals: *Chamaerops humilis, Pinus nigra, wooden sticks*
Non-floral materials: *Candleholder, metal leaf, wire mesh, decorative stars, candle*
How to make it: *For the construction of the sleeve, several green wooden sticks are interwoven into a net for stabilisation and in addition, the Chamaerops-fruits are attached to it with a wire. Fix the pine needles with adhesive spray as well as stick the silvered stars onto the sleeve.*

Zweig/Branch

Seite 30/31:
Werkstoffe: *Pinus strobus, Viscum album*
Materialien: Metall-Hängeleuchter, Draht, Kugeln, Kristalle, Kerzen
Wie wird's gemacht: Mistelzweige in den handelsüblichen Metall-Hängeleuchter hängen bzw. klemmen. Mit Kugeln, Kristallen und Zapfen gleichmäßig schmücken und anschließend die Kerzen auf die vorgesehenen Kerzenteller setzen.
Page 30/31:
Botanicals: Pinus strobus, Viscum album
Non-floral materials: *Hanging metal-candelabra, wire, balls, crystals, candles*
How to make it: *Hang or wedge mistletoes into a usual hanging metal candelabra. Decorate equally with balls, crystals and cones and afterwards put the candles onto the designated candle plates.*

Seite 32:
Werkstoffe: *Viscum album,* Flechte, *Pinus strobus*
Materialien: Steckschaumkugel, Filzband
Wie wird's gemacht: Einen Mistelzweig am Ansatz mit Filzband umwickeln und aufhängen. Steckschaumkugeln werden mit Flechte beklebt und in die Mistelkrone gehängt. Zum Schluss die Zapfen an das herabhängende Ende des Filzbandes knoten.
Page 32:
Botanicals: Viscum album, *lichen*, Pinus strobus
Non-floral materials: *Floral foam ball, felt ribbon*
How to make it: *Decorate the mistletoe with a felt ribbon at the top and suspend. Floral foam balls are pasted with lichen and suspended at the crown of the mistletoe. Finally, knot the cones at the downward flowing end of the felt ribbon.*

Seite 33:
Werkstoffe: *Viscum album,* Flechte, Fasern, Zimtstangen, Apfelscheiben, Ingwer
Materialien: Metallring, Metallkette, Steckschaumkugeln, Kugeln, Rödeldraht
Wie wird's gemacht: Als Aufhängung mehrere Metallketten an dem handelsüblichen Metallring befestigen. Diese Grundkonstruktion dient als Befestigungshilfe für die Mistelzweige, die mit Rödeldraht daran befestigt werden. Anschließend werden an dem Ring entlang die Accessoires wie Zimtstangen, Apfelscheiben, Ingwer und Kugeln geklebt. Zum Schluss die mit Flechte beklebten Steckschaumkugeln auffädeln und an dem Werkstück befestigen.
Page 33:
Botanicals: Viscum album, *lichen, fibres, cinnamon stick, apple slices, ginger*
Non-floral materials: *Metal ring, metal string, floral foam balls, spheres, tie wire*
How to make it: *Attach several metal strings onto the metal ring for the suspension. This base construction serves as an attachment aid for the mistletoes, which are fixed onto it with a wire. Then the accessories, including cinnamon sticks, apple slices, ginger and spheres are stuck along the ring. Finally, the floral foam balls pasted with lichen are threaded and attached to the composition.*

Seite 34/35:
Werkstoffe: *Eucalyptus globulus, Phalaenopsis amabilis, Prunus spinosa, Salix daphnoides, Tillandsia xerographica*
Materialien: Vase, Dekokugeln, Kristalle, Rödeldraht
Wie wird's gemacht: Um die hohe Vase wird oben ein duftiges Nest aus Schlehenzweigen gewunden und mit Rödeldraht fixiert. Dann die Accessoires in den Zweigen befestigen und die *Phalaenopsis* in einem passenden Topfeinsatz oben in die Vase einfügen.
Page 34/35:
Botanicals: Eucalyptus globulus, Phalaenopsis amabilis, Prunus spinosa, Salix daphnoides, Tillandsia xerographica
Non-floral materials: *Vase, decorative balls, crystalls, tie wire*
How to make it: *A loose nest of sloe twigs is twined around the high vase and fixed with tie wire. Then, fix the accessories between the twigs and insert the* Phalaenopsis *planted in an appropriate pot element on the top into the vase.*

Seite 36/37:
Werkstoffe: *Cryptomeria japonica, Lunaria annua, Muehlenbeckia, Senecio cineraria,* Weide, Flechtenzweige, Sisalfasern
Materialien: Spanplatte, Steckschaum, Kristallkugeln, Glasspindeln, Dekosterne, Farbe
Wie wird's gemacht: Als Untergestell für dieses Werkstück dient ein selbst gefertigter Würfel aus Spanplatten, der mit einer Gips-Optik versehen und Steckschaum gefüllt wird. In die obere Platte werden Löcher gebohrt, durch die die Weidenruten gesteckt werden. Sie dienen so als Steckhilfe für die verschiedenen Werkstoffe und Accessoires, die quer dazu eingeschichtet werden.
Page 36/37:
Botanicals: Cryptomeria japonica, Lunaria annua, Muehlenbeckia, Senecio cineraria, *willow, lichen branches, sisal fibres*
Non-floral materials: *Chipboard, floral foam, crystal balls, glass spindles, decorative stars, paint*
How to make it: *The sub-construction of this composition is composed of a self-made cube of chipboard with a gypsum-like look and is filled with floral foam. Holes are drilled into the upper plate into which the osier stakes are put. Thus, they serve as an aid to arrange the various materials and accessories which are added crosswise.*

Seite 38:
Werkstoffe: *Hippeastrum Cultivar, Tillandsia argentea,* Flechtenzweige
Materialien: Vase, Dekosterne, Heißkleber
Wie wird's gemacht: Das breite Gefäß flächendeckend mit Flechtenzweigen bekleben. Zur Akzentuierung Dekosterne anbringen und *Tillandsie* punktuell in die Flechten stecken.
Page 38:
Botanicals: Hippeastrum Cultivar, Tillandsia argentea, *lichen branches*
Non-floral materials: *Vase, decorative stars, hot glue*
How to make it: *Paste the wide container largely with lichen branches. Decorate with stars to accentuate the construction and insert the Tillandsia selectively into the lichen.*

Seite 39:
Werkstoffe: *Fagus sylvatica, Lunaria annua, Muehlenbeckia axillaris, Pinus nigra,* Flechtenzweige
Materialien: Steckschaum, Gefäß, Alustange, Dekosterne, Lichterkette, Kugeln, Sprühkleber, Farbe, Heißkleber
Wie wird's gemacht: Das quadratische Gefäß wird mit Steckschaum gefüllt. Als Bindebasis wird eine lange Alustange in den Steckschaum gesteckt und mit Heißkleber fixiert. Die weiß gefärbten Buchenzweige und die Flechtenzweige jeweils mit einem Ende an die Stange binden, dabei unten beginnen, so dass eine baumähnliche Form entsteht. Zum Schluss die Lichterkette und die Accessoires an den Baum hängen.
Page 39:
Botanicals: Fagus sylvatica, Lunaria annua, Muehlenbeckia axillaris, Pinus nigra, *lichen branches*
Non-floral materials: *Floral foam, container, aluminium rod, decorative stars, Christmas lights, balls, adhesive spray, paint, hot glue*
How to make it: *The square container is filled with floral foam. The binding basis is constructed in the form of a long aluminium rod, which is put into the floral foam and fixed with hot glue. The white coloured birch branches and the lichen branches are tied from the bottom to the top onto the bar with their respective ends, thus creating a tree-like shape. Finally, suspend the Christmas lights and the accessories onto the tree.*

Seite 40/41:
Werkstoffe: *Malus Cultivar, Malus domestica, Pinus sylvestris,* Holzstäbe, Holzklotz
Materialien: Eisenstangen, Rödeldraht, Draht, Kugeln, Glasspindeln, Kerzenhalter, Dekosterne, Kerzen
Wie wird's gemacht: Zwei Eisenstangen in den vorgebohrten Holzklotz stecken. Mit Rödeldraht die Apfel- und Kiefernzweige so daran befestigen, dass ein stabiles Gerüst entsteht. Dann werden die gebleichten Holzstäbe und die restlichen Accessoires eingearbeitet. Zum Schluss die Kerzenhalter auf die Metallstangen stecken und die Kerzen hinzufügen.
Page 40/41:
Botanicals: Malus Cultivar, Malus domestica, Pinus sylvestris, *wooden sticks, log of wood*
Non-floral materials: *Iron bar, tie wire, wire, balls, glass spindles, candleholder, decorative stars, candles*
How to make it: *Insert two iron bars into the predrilled log of wood. Attach the apple and pine twigs onto it with a tie wire creating a stable framework. Then, the bleached wooden sticks and the rest of the accessories are added. At the end, put the candleholders onto the metal rods and add the candles.*

Seite 42:
Werkstoffe: *Alpinia allughas, Eucalyptus globulus, Pinus halepensis, Pinus sylvestris,* Apfelzweigkranz
Materialien: Kerzenhalter, Dekosterne, Kerzen, Dekoäpfel
Wie wird's gemacht: In den handelsüblichen Kranz aus Apfelzweigen werden in regelmäßigen Abständen acht Löcher gebohrt. Dort hinein in gleicher Höhe die Kerzenhalter stecken und mit Heißkleber fixieren. Die restlichen Materialien in den Kranz klemmen, kleben und stecken.
Page 42:
Botanicals: Alpinia allughas, Eucalyptus globulus, Pinus halepensis, Pinus sylvestris, *apple twig wreath*
Non-floral materials: *Candleholder, decorative stars, candles, decorative apples*
How to make it: *Eight regular holes are drilled into the usual wreath of apple twigs. Insert the candleholders into the holes at the same height and fix with hot glue. The rest of the materials is wedged, glued and inserted into the wreath.*

Seite 43:
Werkstoffe: *Helleborus niger, Malus Cultivar, Malus domestica, Pinus sylvestris, Salix daphnoides*
Materialien: Vase, Sand, Rödeldraht, Draht, Dekosterne, Kugeln, Dekoäpfel
Wie wird's gemacht: Eine Vase wird mit Sand gefüllt und ein langer Ast eingesteckt. Daran werden mit Rödeldraht die verschiedenen Zweige so befestigt, dass das Werkstück die Form eines Tannenbaums annimmt. Zum Schluss die Accessoires einhängen und *Helleborus* in die mit Wasser gefüllten Glaskugeln stecken.
Page 43:
Botanicals: Helleborus niger, Malus Cultivar, Malus domestica, Pinus sylvestris, Salix daphnoides
Non-floral materials: *Vase, sand, tie wire, wire, decorative stars, balls, decorative apples*
How to make it: *A vase is filled with sand and a long branch is inserted. The various twigs are attached firmly onto it with the help of a tie wire so that the composition assumes the shape of a fir tree. At the end, suspend the accessories and insert* Helleborus *into the glass balls filled with water.*

Seite 44:
Werkstoffe: *Dipsacus sativus, Leucadendron coniferum, Prunus spinosa*
Materialien: Holzstäbe, Draht, Sprühfarbe, Dekoelemente „Amöben", Glaskugeln
Wie wird's gemacht: Die Schlehenzweige und Holzstäbe werden so senkrecht und waagerecht miteinander verflochten und aneinander gedrahtet, dass das Werkstück eine annähernd kubische Umrissform annimmt und selbstständig steht. Amöben als Stabilisierungshilfe einklemmen und Kugeln und Trockenmaterialien aufkleben.
Page 44:
Botanicals: Dipsacus sativus, Leucadendron coniferum, Prunus spinosa
Non-floral materials: *Wooden sticks, wire, colour spray, decorative elements "amoeba", glass balls*
How to make it: *The sloe branches and the wooden sticks are intertwined vertically and horizontally and wired, thus creating an independent composition with an almost cubic outline. Wedge amoeba to stabilise the composition and stick balls and dry materials onto it.*

Seite 45:
Werkstoffe: *Eucalyptus globulus, Juniperus squamata, Lunaria annua, Prunus spinosa*
Materialien: Vase, Dekosterne, Kugeln, Sternenband, Wachs, Rödeldraht
Wie wird's gemacht: Mit Hilfe von Rödeldraht wird aus den Ästen der Schlehe ein Straußgerüst gefertigt, das anschließend gewachst wird. Dort hinein die Accessoires und den Wacholder arbeiten und das Werkstück zusammen mit einer elektrisch beleuchteten Kugel auf die Vase legen.
Page 45:
Botanicals: Eucalyptus globulus, Juniperus squamata, Lunaria annua, Prunus spinosa
Non-floral materials: *Vase, decorative stars, balls, ribbon with star accessories, wax, tie wire*
How to make it: *A bouquet framework is constructed of the sloe branches with the help of a tie wire and is waxed afterwards. Add the accessories and the juniper into the composition and put on the vase together with an electrically lighted ball.*

Seite 46:
Werkstoffe: *Abies procera 'Glauca'*
Materialien: Vase, Strohkranz, Band, Schmucknadeln, Dekostern, Kugel, Kerzen, Kerzenhalter
Wie wird's gemacht: Der kleine Strohkranz wird mit Vliesband umwickelt. Die Tannenzweige und einige entnadelte Äste werden mit Perlenstecknadeln darauf fixiert und die Kerzen in Kerzenhaltern aufgesteckt. Der Kranz wird auf dem Rand des Gefäßes platziert und seine Öffnung durch eine mit Band und Stern verzierte Dekokugel verschlossen.

Service Service

Page 46:
Botanicals: Abies procera 'Glauca'
Non-floral materials: *Vase, straw wreath, ribbon, decorative pins, decorative star, sphere, candles, candlehodler*
How to make it: *The small straw wreath is wrapped up with a non-woven tape. The fir twigs and some needle-free branches are fixed onto it with the help of pearled pins. Finally, the candles are put into the candleholders. The wreath is placed onto the frame of the container, and a sphere decorated with a ribbon and a star, and finally placed in the middle.*

Seite 47:
Werkstoffe: *Abies procera 'Glauca', Brunia laevis, Chamaerops humilis, Cryptomeria japonica, Euphorbia spinosa, Hydrangea macrophylla, Leucadendron plumosum, Leucophytha brownii, Picea abies, Sempervivum altum, Tillandsia xerographica,* Rinde
Materialien: Steckschaumplatte, Draht, Haften, Kugeln, Pappe, Dekoapfel
Wie wird's gemacht: Die Sternform wird aus einer Steckschaumplatte ausgeschnitten. Die Zacken des Sterns werden anschließend großzügig mit *Nobilis*-Tanne behaftet. Die restliche Fläche wird mit den verschiedenen Werkstoffen und Materialien besteckt. Die Dekosterne sind aus Pappe ausgeschnitten und mit Draht umwickelt.
Page 47:
Botanicals: Abies procera 'Glauca', Brunia laevis, Chamaerops humilis, Cryptomeria japonica, Euphorbia spinosa, Hydrangea macrophylla, Leucadendron plumosum, Leucophytha brownii, Picea abies, Sempervivum altum, Tillandsia xerographica, *bark*
Non-floral materials: *Floral foam board, wire, clamps, balls, cardboard, decorative apple*
How to make it: *The shape of the star is cut out of a floral foam board. The edges of the star are then largely decorated with* Nobilis*-fir. The rest of the surface is adorned with the different botanicals and other materials. The decorative stars are cut out of a cardboard and wrapped up with a wire.*

Seite 48/49:
Werkstoffe: *Abies procera 'Glauca'*
Materialien: Strohrömer, Haften, Schmucknadeln, Kerzenhalter, Kerzen
Wie wird's gemacht: Nobilis-Triebe werden am unteren Ende entnadelt, dann gleichmäßig mit den Spitzen voraus auf einen Strohrömer gehaftet. Das freie, nach außen zeigende untere Triebende wird mit blauen Schmucknadeln versehen. Die ungewöhnliche Verarbeitung der Nobilis macht das Besondere dieses Kerzenkranzes aus, der zum Schluss mit Kerzenhaltern und Kerzen versehen wird.
Page 48/49:
Botanicals: Abies procera 'Glauca'
Non-floral materials: *Straw-base wreath, clamps, decorative pins, candleholder, candles*
How to make it: *The needles of the* Nobilis*-shoots are removed at their lower part, and then attached to a straw base wreath with their points facing upwards. The loose and external end of the shoots is adorned with decorative blue needles. The unusual fabrication of the* Nobilis *creates the unique appearance of this candle wreath. At the end, the wreath is decorated with candleholders and candles.*

Seite 50/51:
Werkstoffe: *Taxus baccata*
Materialien: Steckschaumkranz, Brett, Kerzen, Kugeln
Wie wird's gemacht: Für dieses Kerzenarrangement wird der Steckschaumkranz mit *Taxus* besteckt und auf ein an den Ecken abgerundetes Holzbrett gelegt. Das Innere des Kranzes ist mit Glaskugeln gefüllt.
Page 50/51:
Botanicals: Taxus baccata
Non-floral materials: *Floral foam wreath, board, candles, balls*
How to make it: *The floral foam wreath of this candle arrangement is decorated with Taxus and put on a wooden board, which is rounded at its edges. The interior of the wreath is filled with glass balls.*

Seite 52:
Werkstoffe: *Taxus baccata*
Materialien: Steckschaumkegel, Kerzenleuchter, Kerzen, Dekosterne
Wie wird's gemacht: Basis dieses mit *Taxus* besteckten Bäumchens ist ein Steckschaumkegel. Dieser wird auf einem dreifüßigen Kerzenständer positioniert und mit einem breiten Rand aus aufgenadelten Holzsternen geschmückt.
Page 52:
Botanicals: Taxus baccata
Non-floral materials: *Floral foam cone, candleholder, candles, decorative stars*
How to make it: *The base of this small tree which is adorned with* Taxus *is a floral foam cone which is placed on a tripodal candleholder and decorated with a large frame of pinned wooden stars.*

Seite 53:
Werkstoffe: *Leucadendron sabulosum, Taxus baccata, Sempervivum arachnoideum*
Materialien: Steckschaumkugel, Vase, Schmuckkugeln, Engelshaar, Lichterkette, Holzlocken
Wie wird's gemacht: Eine Steckschaumkugel wird mit Moos bedeckt. Die Holzlocken mal mit einzelnen Lichtern einer Lichterkette, mal mit Schmuckkugeln, Zapfen oder *Taxus* füllen und in gleichmäßiger Verteilung dicht an dicht auf die Steckschaumkugel stecken.
Page 53:
Botanicals: Leucadendron sabulosum, Taxus baccata, Sempervivum arachnoideum
Non-floral materials: *Floral foam ball, vase, Christmas balls, angel hair, Christmas lights, wooden curls*
How to make it: *A floral foam ball is covered with moss. Fill the wooden curls alternately with single layers of Christmas lights and decorative balls, cones or Taxus and attach equally and in a dense arrangement onto the floral foam ball.*

Seite 54/55:
Werkstoffe: *Thuja plicata, Pinus strobus*
Materialien: Kerzenständer, Draht, Kerzen, Dekosterne, Hörner, Geweihstangen
Wie wird's gemacht: Die Kerzenständer werden mit Zweigen der *Thuja* und trockenen Ästen umwickelt und mit Draht fixiert. Hörner, Geweihstangen, Zapfen und die Dekosterne dazwischenklemmen und anschließend die Stumpenkerzen einsetzen.
Page 54/55:
Botanicals: Thuja plicata, Pinus strobus
Non-floral materials: *Candleholder, wire, candles, decorative stars, horns, antler*
How to make it: *The candleholder is wrapped up with the* Thuja *twigs and dry branches, and then fixed with a wire. Wedge the horns, antlers, cones and the decorative stars in-between and insert the pillar candles thereafter.*

Seite 56/57:
Werkstoffe: *Cornus alba 'Sibirica', Ilex aquifolium, Pinus nigra, Rudbeckia fulgida,* Balani-Scheiben, Zimtstangen
Materialien: Ballierungsnetze, Riedbunde, rot lackiertes Papprohr, Dekosterne
Wie wird's gemacht: Ober- und unterhalb eines ca. 15 cm langen Papprohres, das an den Rändern mit Löchern versehen ist, werden zwei Ballierungsnetze angedrahtet. Die mit Rödeldraht aneinander befestigten Riedstäbe und *Cornus*-Zweige werden dann durch die Netze geflochten und eingeklemmt. Dann werden die Accessoires angedrahtet und im Werkstück befestigt.
Page 56/57:
Botanicals: Cornus alba 'Sibirica', Ilex aquifolium, Pinus nigra, Rudbeckia fulgida, *Balani-discs, cinnamon-sticks*
Non-floral materials: *Wire mesh, reed bunches, red varnished cardboard pipe, decorative stars*
How to make it: *A cardboard pipe measuring 15 cm in length which has holes drilled in its ends is wired with two wire meshes. The reed sticks and Cornus-twigs which are fixed with each other with the help of a tie wire are intertwined and wedged into these baskets. Finally, the accessories are wired and attached to the composition.*

Seite 58:
Werkstoffe: *Banksia grandis, Cornus alba, Datura ceratocaula, Pinus nigra,* Hagebutten
Materialien: Holzplatten, Metallstangen, Rödeldraht, Kugeln, Kerzen, Dekoelemente „Amöbe"
Wie wird's gemacht: Aus den Holzplatten und den Metallstangen einen sicher stehenden Ständer bauen. Die *Cornus* und Kiefern-Zweige mit Rödeldraht quer an den Metallstangen befestigen. Als schmückende Elemente werden Kugeln, Amöben, Stechapfel und *Banksia* eingearbeitet. Zum Schluss mehrere rote Stumpenkerzen auf die Platte stellen.
Page 58:
Botanicals: Banksia grandis, Cornus alba, Datura ceratocaula, Pinus nigra, *rosehips*
Non-floral materials: *Wooden plates, metal rods, tie wire, balls, candles, decorative elements "Amoeba"*
How to make it: *Construct a stable stand out of the wooden plates and the metal rods. Attach the* Cornus *and pine-twigs with the help of a tie wire crosswise onto the metal rods. The decorative materials used include balls, amoeba, Thorn apple and* Banksia*. At the end, place several red pillar candles onto the board.*

Seite 59:
Werkstoffe: *Cornus alba 'Sibirica', Hippeastrum vittatum, Ilex verticillata, Pinus pinea, Punica granatum,* Gewürznelken
Materialien: Holzbrett, Metallstangen, Rödeldraht, Dekosterne, Band
Wie wird's gemacht: In ein schwarz gestrichenes Holzbrett werden in Kreisform Löcher gebohrt, in denen lange Metallstangen Halt finden. Zwischen den Stangen hindurch wird ein Kranz aus Hartriegel gefertigt, der mit Rödeldraht fixiert ist. Zusätzlich die *Ilex*-Beeren mit Draht im Kranz befestigen. Zapfen und Granatäpfel werden auf die Metallstangen gesteckt und die Dekosterne an langen Bändern an den Kranz gehängt. Zum Schluss die Amaryllispflanzen mit ihren ausgewaschenen Zwiebeln auf der Bodenplatte platzieren.
Page 59:
Botanicals: Cornus alba 'Sibirica', Hippeastrum vittatum, Ilex verticillata, Pinus pinea, Punica granatum, *cloves*
Non-floral materials: *Wooden board, metal rods, tie wire, decorative stars, ribbon*
How to make it: *Holes are drilled in a circular shape into a black painted wooden board into which long metal sticks are inserted. A wreath made of Cornus is constructed between these sticks and fixed with a tie wire. In addition, attach the* Ilex*-berries onto the wreath with the help of a wire. The cones and pomegranates are put on top of the metal sticks and the decorative stars are suspended at the wreath on long ribbons. At the end, place the Amaryllis plants with their washed-out bulbs onto the base plate.*

Seite 60:
Werkstoffe: *Aegle marmelos, Bertholettia excelsa, Ligustrum vulgare, Thuja plicata, Pinus nigra,* Moos
Materialien: Schale, Gestell mit Kerzenhalter, Stäbe, Kugeln, Kerzen, Hörner
Wie wird's gemacht: Das handelsübliche Gestell mit den Kerzenhaltern in einer runden Schale fixieren und die *Thuja*-Zweige durch das Gestell flechten. Zusätzlich die farbigen Stäbe kreuz und quer einarbeiten. Die Mitte der Schale wird mit Moos aufgefüllt und Liguster, Kugeln und die Trockenfrüchte darauf arrangiert.
Page 60:
Botanicals: Aegle marmelos, Bertholettia excelsa, Ligustrum vulgare, Thuja plicata, Pinus nigra, *moss*
Non-floral materials: *Bowl, framework with candleholder, sticks, balls, candles, horns*
How to make it: *Fix the usual stand with the candleholders into a round bowl and braid the Thuja-twigs through this stand. In addition, integrate the coloured sticks irregularly. The middle of the bowl is filled with moss and adorned with privet, balls and dry fruits.*

Seite 61:
Werkstoffe: *Helleborus niger, Ilex verticillata, Scabiosa stellata, Thuja plicata*
Materialien: Schale, Dekosterne, Kugeln, Hörner, Geweihstangen
Wie wird's gemacht: Die Schale mit senkrecht mit kurzen, entzweigten *Thuja*-Ästen füllen, die anderen Werkstoffe wie *Ilex* und *Scabiosa* dazwischen stecken. Als Schmuckelemente Kugeln und Dekosterne hinzufügen.
Page 61:
Botanicals: Helleborus niger, Ilex verticillata, Scabiosa stellata, Thuja plicata
Non-floral materials: *Bowl, decorative stars, balls, horns, antler*
How to make it: *Fill the bowl with vertical, short twig-free* Thuja*-branches, and put the other botanicals like Ilex and Scabiosa in-between. Add balls and stars as decorative elements.*

Seite 62/63:
Werkstoffe: *Pinus mugo, Pinus pinea*
Materialien: Schale, Draht, Band, Sterne
Wie wird's gemacht: Über den aus Kiefernzweigen gebundenen Strauß werden zusätzliche Zweige quer gelegt und mit Papierdraht befestigt. Die großen Sterne aus gefärbter Pappe sind aufgeklebt.
Page 62/63:
Botanicals: Pinus mugo, Pinus pinea
Non-floral materials: *Bowl, wire, ribbon, stars*
How to make it: *Additional twigs are laid crosswise above the bunch of pine twigs tied together in the form of a bouquet and attached with a paper wire. The big stars of coloured cardboard are glued onto the bouquet.*

Seite 64:
Werkstoffe: *Malus pumila, Muehlenbeckia axillaris, Pinus cembra, Pinus nigra,* Moos
Materialien: Gefäß, Draht, Kugeln, Band, Dekosterne, Lichterkette, Steine
Wie wird's gemacht: Mit Hilfe von Steinen wird der Holzstamm fest in dem Gefäß eingeklemmt. Dann die Steine mit Moos abdecken. Mit Mühlenbeckie die Grundform in Gestalt eines Baumes um den Stamm wickeln und die Lichterkette daran befestigen. Zusätzlich werden die Kiefernzweige kreuz und quer eingesteckt und mit Draht fixiert. Zum Schluss die Accessoires in den Baum hängen.
Page 64:
Botanicals: Malus pumila, Muehlenbeckia axillaris, Pinus cembra, Pinus nigra, *moss*
Non-floral materials: *Container, wire, balls, ribbon, decorative stars, Christmas stars, stones*
How to make it: *The log is firmly wedged into the container with the help of stones. Then cover the stones with moss. Wrap Muehlenbeckia around the log creating the shape of a tree as the base of this construction and fix the Christmas lights onto it. The pine needles are additionally inserted here and there and fixed with a wire. At the end, hook the accessories into the tree.*

Seite 65:
Werkstoffe: *Pinus mugo*
Materialien: Kerzenhalter, Holzreif, Brett, Tonkinstäbe, Rödeldraht, Engel, Kerzen
Wie wird's gemacht: Mit Rödeldraht werden die Kiefernzweige auf einem Holzreif befestigt. Dann in ein Holzbrett Löcher bohren, die Tonkinstäbe darin einstecken und den Kiefernkranz hieran festdrahten. Die Kerzenhalter werden auf die Stäbe geklebt.
Page 65:
Botanicals: Pinus mugo
Non-floral materials: *Candleholder, wooden circlet, board, Tonkin-sticks, tie wire, angel, candles*
How to make it: *The pine twigs are fixed onto a wooden circlet with the help of a tie wire. Then drill holes into a wooden board, insert the Tonkin-sticks and wire the pine wreath onto these sticks. The candleholders are stuck onto the sticks.*

Seite 66/67:
Werkstoffe: *Cupressus arizonica, Pinus strobus,* Kokos-Brakteen
Materialien: Brett, Alustangen, Kabelbinder, Kerzenhalter, Dekosterne, Kugeln, Kerzen, Dekoäpfel
Wie wird's gemacht: In das rot gestrichene Holzbrett werden in gleichmäßigen Abständen vier Löcher gebohrt. Darin werden die hohlen Alustangen festgeklemmt. Die Sterne, Äpfel und Kokos-Brakteen mittig durchbohren und über die Alustangen schieben. Zweige und die restlichen Accessoires mit Kabelbindern befestigen. Zum Schluss die Kerzenhalter oben in die Alustangen stecken und mit den Kerzen versehen.
Page 66/67:
Botanicals: Cupressus arizonica, Pinus strobus, *Coco-bracts*
Non-floral materials: *Board, aluminium sticks, binder, candleholder, decorative stars, balls, candles, decorative apples*
How to make it: *Four spaced holes are drilled into a red painted wooden board into which the hollow aluminium rods are wedged.*

Wie wird's gemacht: Auf den Rebstock wird Heu in Form eines Baumes gewickelt und mit Draht fixiert. Die Zapfen aufkleben und das Werkstück in den Topf stecken. Der Steckschaum wird mit Lappenmoos abgedeckt.
Page 105:
Botanicals: Cupressus sempervirens, *moss, vine, straw*
Non-floral materials: *Container, floral foam, decorative star, wire*
How to make it: *The vine is wrapped up with straw in the form of a tree and fixed with a wire. Stick the cones onto and put the composition into the pot. The floral foam is covered with sheet moss*

Seite 106/107:
Werkstoffe: *Malus Cultivar, Pinus mugo, Pinus strobus, Pinus wallichiana,* Moos
Materialien: Steckschaumkranz, Schale
Wie wird's gemacht: Der Steckschaumkranz wird zuerst mit Moos bedeckt und dann mit angedrahteten Zapfen besteckt. Anschließend die Kiefernnadeln zwischen die Zapfen stecken. Zur besonderen Betonung können Zieräpfel rund um den Kranz gelegt werden.
Page 106/107:
Botanicals: Malus Cultivar, Pinus mugo, Pinus strobus, Pinus wallichiana, *moss*
Non-floral materials: *Floral foam wreath, bowl*
How to make it: *At first, the floral foam wreath is covered with moss and then decorated with the wired cones. Then insert the pine needles between the cones. For a particular accentuation, the decorative apples can be laid around the wreath.*

Seite 108:
Werkstoffe: *Cornus alba 'Sibirica', Crataegus laevigata, Ginkgo biloba, Malus Cultivar, Pinus nigra, Pinus pinea*
Materialien: Metallfuß, Filzband, Dekostern, Krampen
Wie wird's gemacht: In den Ast unten ein Loch bohren und diesen dann auf den Dorn eines handelsüblichen Metallfußes setzen. Zusätzlich die *Cornus*-Zweige quer dazu mit Draht in dem Zweig befestigen und mit *Malus* behängen. In die Zapfen wird jeweils eine Krampe gehämmert, damit sie an Bändern befestigt und angehängt werden können.
Page 108:
Botanicals: Cornus alba 'Sibirica', Crataegus laevigata, Ginkgo biloba, Malus Cultivar, Pinus nigra, Pinus pinea
Non-floral materials: *Metal foot, felt ribbon, decorative star, cramps*
How to make it: *Drill a hole into the bottom side of the branch and place onto the pin of a usual metal foot. In addition, fix the* Cornus*-branches horizontally onto the twig with the help of a wire and decorate with* Malus*. A cramp is hammered into each cone to attach them with ribbons onto which they are suspended.*

Seite 109:
Werkstoffe: *Pinus mugo, Pinus wallichiana, Viscum album,* Holzstücke
Materialien: Band, Dekostern, Wachs
Wie wird's gemacht:
Flüssiges Wachs in einer entsprechenden Form zu einer rechteckigen Platte gießen und die verschiedenen Werkstoffe hineinlegen. Sobald der Wachs ausgekühlt ist, wird die Form so lange in heißes Wasser gelegt, bis sich das Wachsbild gelöst hat.
Page 109:
Botanicals: Pinus mugo, Pinus wallichiana, Viscum album, *wooden pieces*
Non-floral materials: *Ribbon, decorative star, wax*
How to make it: *Fill a rectangular plate with liquid wax and insert the different materials. After the wax has cooled down, the plate is put into hot water until the wax has dissolved.*

Seite 110:
Werkstoffe: *Arctium minus, Ilex verticillata, Malus Cultivar, Punica granatum, Pinus nigra, Pinus wallichiana, Viscum album,* Moos
Materialien: Gefäß, Steckschaumzylinder, Lichterkette, Kugeln, Band, Dekostern
Wie wird's gemacht: Der Steckschaumzylinder wird in das Gefäß gesetzt und mit Moos bewickelt. Anschließend zuerst die angedrahteten Zapfen um den Rand des Gefäßes geordnet in den Steckschaum stecken, dann die Lichterkette einarbeiten. Zum Schluss die übrigen Werkstoffe und Materialien andrahten und einstecken bzw. direkt einstecken.
Page 110:
Botanicals: Arctium minus, Ilex verticillata, Malus Cultivar, Punica granatum, Pinus nigra, Pinus wallichiana, Viscum album, *moss*
Non-floral materials: *Container, floral foam cone, Christmas lights, balls, ribbon, decorative star*
How to make it: *The floral foam cone is put into the container and wrapped up with moss. Then, insert the wired cones around the rim of the container into the floral foam and add the lights. At the end, wire the rest of the materials and insert or add immediately without any wiring.*

Seite 111:
Werkstoffe: *Crataegus laevigata, Pinus mugo, Stachys byzantina,* Moos
Materialien: Steckschaumkugel, Draht, Holzklotz, Dekostern
Wie wird's gemacht: Die angedrahteten Zapfen werden in die mit Moos bewickelte Steckschaumkugel gesteckt. Diese wiederum wird auf einem Nagel fixiert, der vorher in den Holzklotz geschlagen wurde. Die Zweige werden seitlich an den Holzklotz gebohrt und mit Dekosternen und *Stachys*-Blättern behangen.
Page 111:
Botanicals: Crataegus laevigata, Pinus mugo, Stachys byzantina, *moss*
Non-floral materials: *Floral foam ball, wire, wooden brick, decorative star*
How to make it: *The wired cones are put into the floral foam ball wrapped up with moss which is fixed onto a nail previously driven into the wooden brick. The twigs are drilled at the side of the wooden brick and adorned with decorative stars and* Stachys*-leaves.*

Blatt/*Leaf*

Seite 114/115:
Werkstoffe: *Stachys byzantina*
Materialien: Strohrömer, doppelseitiges Klebeband, Draht, Kerzenhalter, Kerzen, Dekosterne
Wie wird's gemacht: Der Strohrömer wird mit doppelseitigem Klebeband beklebt, auf dem dann die *Stachys*-Blätter gleichmäßig dachziegelartig angebracht werden. Aus Draht ein Geflecht in Ringform fertigen, Dekosterne aufkleben und auf dem Kranz fixieren. Zum Schluss die Kerzen mit Kerzenhaltern befestigen.
Page 114/115:
Botanicals: Stachys byzantina
Non-floral materials: *Straw base wreath, double sided adhesive tape, wire, candleholder, candles, and decorative stars*
How to make it: *Double adhesive tape ist put on the straw base wreath, onto which the* Stachys*-leaves are put in a regular and imbricate arrangement. Construct a trestle out of wire in the form of a circle, stick the decorative stars onto and fix onto the wreath. At the end, place the candles with their sticks.*

Seite 116/117:
Werkstoffe: *Ceropegia linearis subsp. woodii, Eucalyptus polyanthemos, Lavandula angustifolia, Stachys byzantina*
Materialien: Steckschaumkugel, Draht, LED-Lichterkette, Stecknadeln, Dekosterne, Kunstschneematte
Wie wird's gemacht: Die Steckschaumkugel wird durch einen wellenlinienförmigen Schnitt in zwei Teile geteilt. Beide Hälften anschließend aushöhlen und von außen mittels Stecknadeln mit *Stachys*-Blättern bestecken. Das ausgehöhlte Innere der beiden Hälften wird mit einer Kunstschneematte beklebt und schließlich mit der Lichterkette gefüllt. Eingesteckte Holzstäbe dienen als Abstandshalter. Der Zwischenraum, der so entsteht, wenn die beiden Hälften wieder aufeinander gesetzt werden, wird mit Draht, *Eucalyptus, Lavandula* und den Accessoires gefüllt.
Page 116/117:
Botanicals: Ceropegia linearis subsp. woodii, Eucalyptus polyanthemos, Lavandula angustifolia, Stachys byzantina
Non-floral materials: *Floral foam ball, wire, LED-lights, pins, decorative stars, mat of artificial snow*
How to make it: *The floral foam ball is divided into two parts through an undulated cut. Both parts are then hollowed out and adorned with* Stachys*-leaves from the outside with the help of pins. The hollowed interior of the semi balls is pasted with a mat of artificial snow and finally filled with the Christmas lights. Inserted wooden sticks serve as spacers. The gap, which is created when the two parts are put together, is filled with wire,* Eucalyptus, Lavandula *and the accessories.*

Seite 118/119:
Werkstoffe: *Eucalyptus polyanthemos,* Holzscheiben, Anisfrüchte
Materialien: Steckschaumkugeln, Engelshaar, Glaskugeln, Stecknadeln, Wachs
Wie wird's gemacht: Drei der sieben Steckschaumkugeln sind mit *Eucalyptus* besteckt. Die anderen werden jeweils mit Anisfrüchten, Holzscheiben oder mit den Scherben von Glaskugeln beklebt. Die Kugel vorne rechts im Bild ist mit silbernem Engelshaar beklebt und anschließend mit Wachs bestrichen worden.
Page 118/119:
Botanicals: Eucalyptus polyanthemos, *wooden discs, anise fruits*
Non-floral materials: *Floral foam balls, angel hair, glass balls, pins, wax*
How to make it: *Three of the seven floral foam balls are decorated with* Eucalyptus*. The rest is pasted with anise fruits, wooden discs or with fragments of glass balls. The ball in the front to the right is pasted with silvery angel hair and then coated with wax.*

Seite 120/121:
Werkstoffe: *Chrysanthemum x grandiflorum, Dianthus caryophyllus, Eucalyptus polyanthemos, Helleborus niger, Lavandula angustifolia*
Materialien: Gefäße, Frischsteckschaum-Kugel, doppelseitiges Klebeband, Draht, Schlagmetall, Dekosterne, Kugeln, Engelshaar, Blei
Wie wird's gemacht: Vier Kunststoffgefäße werden mit doppelseitigem Klebeband beklebt und *Eucalyptus*-Blätter darauf befestigt. Für das linke Werkstück werden Nelken Kopf an Kopf in eine Frischsteckschaum-Kugel gesteckt. Dann wird die Kugel auf das Gefäß gelegt und mit Engelshaar akzentuiert wird. Bei dem zweiten Werkstück wird eine Glaskugel mit der Öffnung nach oben auf das mit Steckschaum gefüllte Gefäß gelegt. Der Zwischenraum wird mit *Lavandula*-Zweigen, *Eucalyptus*-Fruchtständen, Engelshaar und Zierdraht gefüllt. Die Steckschaumkugel im dritten Gefäß wird mit *Eucalyptus*-Blütenständen und Zierdraht umwickelt. Hier sind wenige Blätter mit Schlagmetall veredelt. Ganz rechts schmücken Kopf an Kopf in die Frischsteckschaum-Kugel gesteckte Chrysanthemen das Gefäß.
Page 120/121:
Botanicals: Chrysanthemum x grandiflorum, Dianthus caryophyllus, Eucalyptus polyanthemos, Helleborus niger, Lavandula angustifolia
Non-floral materials: *Container, fresh floral foam ball, double adhesive tape, wire, metal leaf, decorative stars, balls, angel hair, lead*
How to make it: *Four plastic containers are pasted with a double adhesive tape and the* Eucalyptus*-leaves are attached onto it. For the composition on the left the carnation is put into a fresh floral foam ball in a head-to-head arrangement. Then the ball is placed on the container and decorated left with angel hair. For the second composition an open glass ball is put on a container filled with floral foam. The gap is filled with* Lavandula*-twigs,* Eucalyptus*-infructescenes, angel hair and decorative wire. The floral foam ball in the third container is wrapped up with* Eucalyptus*-inflorescences and a decorative wire. In this example only few leaves are decorated with metal leaf. The container presented on the far right is adorned with* Chrysanthemum *which are inserted in a head-to-head arrangement into the floral foam.*

Seite 122/123:
Werkstoffe: *Hedera helix*
Materialien: Strohrömer, Haften, Kerzenhalter, Filzband, Dekosterne, Kerzen
Wie wird's gemacht: *Hedera*-Blätter werden zu Bündeln gefasst und an der Blattbasis so auf einen Strohrömer gehaftet, dass die Blattstiele in alle Richtungen herausschauen. Die eingesteckten Kerzenhalter sind durch Schnecken aus rotem Filzband verdeckt.
Page 122/123:
Botanicals: Hedera helix
Non-floral materials: *Straw-base wreath, clamps, candlestick, felt ribbon, decorative stars, candles*
How to make it: Hedera*-leaves are put in bunches and thus attached to the straw-base wreath at the leaf base so that the petioles stick out in all directions. The inserted candlesticks are covered with felt ribbon wrapped around in a spiral.*

Seite 124/125:
Werkstoffe: *Hedera helix, Lavandula angustifolia,* Moos, *Pinus mugo,* Rinde, Zimtstangen, Anis, Belani-Scheiben
Materialien: Gefäß, Steckschaum, Tonpappe, Spiegelbeeren, Dekosterne, Woll-Pompon
Wie wird's gemacht: Aus Tonpappe eine Manschette formen und mit Kleber fixieren. An der unteren Seite Zacken einschneiden und dann die Pappe mit doppelseitigem Klebeband bekleben. Darauf werden die *Hedera*-Blätter geklebt. Diese *Hedera*-Manschette auf das mit Steckschaum gefüllte Gefäß legen und schließlich von oben mit den Werkstoffen bestecken.
Page 124/125:
Botanicals: Hedera helix, Lavandula angustifolia, *moss,* Pinus mugo, *bark, cinnamon sticks, anise, Belani-discs*
Non-floral materials: *Container, floral foam, cardboard, glass berries, decorative stars, woollen pompon*
How to make it: *Form a sleeve out of cardboard and fix with glue. Cut jags into the lower side and then paste the cardboard with double adhesive tape. The* Hedera*-leaves are stuck onto it. Put this* Hedera*-sleeve onto the container filled with floral foam and finally decorate the surface with floral foam.*

Seite 126/127:
Werkstoffe: *Ilex aquifolium, Malus Cultivar*
Materialien: Metallständer, Draht, Kranzband, Stecknadeln, Heu
Wie wird's gemacht: Der Metallständer wird mit Steckdraht verlängert und anschließend mit Hilfe von Draht mit Heu umwickelt, das dann zu einer Tüte geformt wird. Um Stabilität zu erreichen, wird es anschließend mit Kranzband umwickelt und die *Ilex*-Blätter mit Stecknadeln auf der Oberfläche befestigt.
Page 126/127:
Botanicals: Ilex aquifolium, Malus Cultivar
Non-floral materials: *Metal stand, wire, wreath ribbon, pins, straw*
How to make it: *The metal stand is extended by a florist wire and then wrapped up with straw with the help of a wire which is finally formed in the shape of a cone. To obtain stability it is wrapped up with a wreath ribbon and the* Ilex*-leaves are attached onto the surface with the help of pins.*

Seite 128/129:
Werkstoffe: *Ilex aquifolium, Pinus*-Zapfen, Aststück
Materialien: Gefäß, doppelseitiges Klebeband, Kreppband, Kugeln, Kerze
Wie wird's gemacht: Damit die Schale später wieder verwendet werden kann, wird sie zuerst mit Kreppband umwickelt. Anschließend wird darüber doppelseitiges Klebeband geklebt und die *Ilex*-Blätter darauf befestigt. Nun wird sie mit dem Aststück, den Accessoires und Kerzen gefüllt.
Page 128/129:
Botanicals: Ilex aquifolium, Pinus-cones, *piece of branch*
Non-floral materials: *Container, double adhesive tape, crepe ribbon, balls, candles*
How to make it: *At first the bowl is wrapped up with crepe ribbon to make a further use possible. Then it is pasted with double adhesive tape and the* Ilex*-leaves are fixed onto it. Finally, it is filled with pieces of branch, the accessories and the candles.*

Blüte/*Flower*

Seite 132/133:
Werkstoffe: *Betula pendula, Cedrus atlantica, Helleborus niger, Salix caprea*
Materialien: Kerzenleuchter, Draht, Glasröhrchen, Kugeln, Dekosterne, Kerzen
Wie wird's gemacht: Die *Betula*-Zweige werden weiß gestrichen und dann so mit Draht an dem Kerzenleuchter befestigt, dass ein Gerüst entsteht. Die verschiedenen Werkstoffe einklemmen und die Wasserröhrchen für die Christrosen mit Draht in dem Gerüst befestigen. Zum Schluss die angedrahteten Accessoires einarbeiten.
Page 132/133:
Botanicals: Betula pendula, Cedrus atlantica, Helleborus niger, Salix caprea

Non-floral materials: *Candelabra, wire, glass tubes, balls, decorative stars, candles*
How to make it: *The Betula-twigs are painted in white and then attached to the candelabra thus creating a framework. Wedge the different materials into it and fix the water tubes for the* Helleborus *within the framework. At the end, add the wired accessories.*

Seite 134:
Werkstoffe: *Betula pendula, Helleborus niger*
Materialien: Stoffserviette, Glasröhrchen, Dekosterne
Wie wird's gemacht: Die Serviette wird erst zu einem Dreieck zusammengelegt. Nun werden die unteren Ränder umgelegt. Anschließend die Serviette zusammenrollen und weiß gestrichene *Betula*-Zweige einstecken. Zum Schluss das Röhrchen mit der Christrose hinein legen.
Page 134:
Botanicals: Betula pendula, Helleborus niger
Non-floral materials: *Napkin decoration, glass tubes, decorative stars*
How to make it: *First the napkin is folded in the form of a triangle. Then, the lower edges are turned, the napkin is rolled and the* Betula*-twigs are inserted. Finally, put the tube containing the* Helleborus *into the napkin.*

Seite 135 oben:
Werkstoffe: *Betula pendula, Cedrus atlantica, Helleborus niger*
Materialien: Gefäß, Seidenmalfarbe
Wie wird's gemacht: Die *Betula*-Zweige werden auf gleiche Länge gekürzt, weiß gestrichen und in ein Gefäß, das zu einem Drittel mit weiß gefärbtem Wasser gefüllt ist, gestellt. Anschließend *Helleborus* und *Cedrus* einstellen.
Page 135 top picture:
Botanicals: Betula pendula, Cedrus atlantica, Helleborus niger
Non-floral materials: *Container, silk paint*
How to make it: *The* Betula*-twigs are cut in the same length, painted in white and put into a container, of which a third is filled with white coloured water. Then insert* Helleborus *and* Cedrus.

Seite 135 unten:
Werkstoffe: *Betula pendula, Cedrus atlantica, Helleborus niger, Salix caprea, Malus Cultivar*
Materialien: Gefäß, Dekostern, Kunstschnee, Eiszapfen
Wie wird's gemacht: Aus den auf gleiche Länge gekürzten und zum Teil weiß gestrichenen Zweigen wird mit Hilfe von Silberdraht ein Gerüst gefertigt. Das Gefäß mit Wasser füllen und mit Kunstschnee und dem gewachsten Apfel füllen. Zum Schluss die Christrosen durch das Zweiggerüst stecken.
Page 135 bottom picture:
Botanicals: Betula pendula, Cedrus atlantica, Helleborus niger, Salix caprea, Malus Cultivar
Non-floral materials: *Container, decorative star, artificial snow, icicle*
How to make it: *A framework is constructed of the white-painted and equally cut twigs with the help of a silver wire. Fill the container with water, artificial snow and the waxed apple. At the end, insert the* Helleborus *through the branch framework.*

Seite 136: Werkstoffe: *Cedrus atlantica, Eucharis amazonica*
Materialien: Gefäß, Draht, Stäbe, Dekostern, Glas-Eiszapfen
Wie wird's gemacht: Die weißen Stäbe werden an einer Seite zu einem Bündel zusammengebunden. Dieses wird so in der Vase arrangiert, dass ein paar Stäbe von außen an der Vase entlang laufen. Die Accessoires werden angedrahtet und an den Stäben befestigt.
Page 136:
Botanicals: Cedrus atlantica, Eucharis amazonica
Non-floral materials: *Container, wire, sticks, decorative star, glass-icicles*
How to make it: *The white sticks are tied together in the form of a bundle which is put into the vase with some of them sticking out. The accessories are wired and attached to the sticks.*

Seite 137:
Werkstoffe: *Cedrus atlantica, Eucharis amazonica, Euphorbia spinosa*
Materialien: Gefäß, Draht, Stäbe, Dekostern, Glas-Eiszapfen
Wie wird's gemacht: *Euphorbia* wird quer auf das Gefäß gelegt und dient so als Steckhilfe für *Eucharis* und *Cedrus*. Die Stäbe werden anschließend quer durch das Gestell gezogen und die Accessoires mit Draht befestigt.
Page 137:
Botanicals: Cedrus atlantica, Eucharis amazonica, Euphorbia spinosa
Non-floral materials: *Container, wire, sticks, decorative star, glass-icicles*
How to make it: Euphorbia *is laid around the container and serves as an aid for arranging* Eucharis *and* Cedrus. *Then the sticks are threaded through the framework and the accessories fixed with a wire.*

Seite 138:
Werkstoffe: *Berzelia lanuginosa, Euphorbia spinosa, Leucadendon coniferum, Leucadendron laureolum, Leucospermum cordifolium, Pinus mugo, Protea barbigera, Punica granatum*
Materialien: Gefäß, Dekosterne, Geweihstangen
Wie wird's gemacht: Zweige werden angedrahtet und kreuz und quer zu einem Gerüst zusammengebunden. Die Werkstoffe werden dann nach und nach eingefügt bzw. eingebunden.
Page 138:
Botanicals: Berzelia lanuginosa, Euphorbia spinosa, Leucadendon coniferum, Leucadendron laureolum, Leucospermum cordifolium, Pinus mugo, Protea barbigera, Punica granatum

Non-floral materials: *Container, decorative stars, horns*
How to make it: *Twigs are wired and irregularly tied together in the form of a framework. The materials are inserted bit by bit or tied into.*

Seite 139:
Werkstoffe: *Eucalyptus globulus, Pinus mugo, Protea barbigera,* Birkenrindenplatten
Materialien: Gefäß, Steckschaum, Dekosterne, Kugeln
Wie wird's gemacht: In das quadratische Gefäß werden zur Erhöhung der Wandungen handelsübliche und passend zurechtgeschnittene Birkenrindenplatten geklemmt. Anschließend das Innere des Gefäßes mit Steckschaum füllen und die *Protea* zusammen mit den anderen Werkstoffen einstecken.
Page 139:
Botanicals: Eucalyptus globulus, Pinus mugo, Protea barbigera, *Birch bark plates*
Non-floral materials: *Container, floral foam, decorative stars, balls*
How to make it: *Usual birch bark plates, which are appropriately cut, are wedged into the square container in order to extend its walls. Then fill the interior of the container with floral foam and insert the* Protea *together with the rest of the materials.*

Seite 140/141:
Werkstoffe: *Cattleya Cultivar, Chamaerops humilis, Eucalyptus polyanthemos, Ligustrum vulgare, Miltoniopsis Cultivar, Musa x paradisiaca, Phalaenopsis amabilis, Picea abies, Punica granatum, Rosa Cultivar, Tillandsia x Vuylstekeara Cultivar, Zantedeschia rehmannii,* Moos
Materialien: Steckschaum, Kugeln, Glasröhrchen, Geweihstangen
Wie wird's gemacht:
Eine Unterlage aus Steckschaum zurechtschneiden mit Tonkinstäben zusammenfügen von unten mit Hartschaumunterlage stabilisieren. Zusätzlich alles mit Folie und mit Moos abdecken. Die Zapfen andrahten und rings herum seitlich in den Steckschaum stecken. Anschließend die Steckunterlage mit Orchideen in Wasserröhrchen und weiteren Werkstoffen ausstecken. Die Accessoires werden andrahtet und ebenfalls hinzugefügt.
Page 140/141:
Botanicals: Cattleya Cultivar, Chamaerops humilis, Eucalyptus polyanthemos, Ligustrum vulgare, Miltoniopsis Cultivar, Musa x paradisiaca, Phalaenopsis amabilis, Picea abies, Punica granatum, Rosa Cultivar, Tillandsia x Vuylstekeara Cultivar, Zantedeschia rehmannii, *moss*
Non-floral materials: *Floral foam, balls, glass tubes, horns*
How to make it: *Cut a base out of floral foam, combine with Tonkin sticks and support with a hard floral foam base from below. Cover everything additionally with foil and moss. Wire the cones and insert laterally into the floral foam. Then decorate the floral foam base with water tubes filled with orchids and other botanicals. The accessories are wired and also added.*

Seite 142:
Werkstoffe: *Phalaenopsis Cultivar, Pinus radiata,* Zimtstangen
Materialien: Glasröhrchen, Filzband
Wie wird's gemacht: Das Glasröhrchen wird mit Kiefernnadeln ummantelt. Die Bindestelle mit dem Filzband verdecken und die Orchidee in das Röhrchen stecken.
Page 142:
Botanicals: Phalaenopsis Cultivar, Pinus radiata, *cinnamon sticks*
Non-floral materials: *Glass tubes, felt ribbon*
How to make it: *The glass tube is wrapped up with pine needles. Cover the binding point with the felt ribbon and insert the orchid into the tube.*

Seite 143 oben:
Werkstoffe: *Chamaerops humilis, Olea europaea, Pinus pinea, Punica granatum, x Vuylstekeara Cultivar*
Materialien: Holzfuß, Holzstab, Holzkugel, Dekostern
Wie wird's gemacht: In den Holzfuß mittig ein Loch bohren, in das ein Holzstab geklebt wird. Die Werkstoffe und Accessoires werden anschließend nacheinander aufspießt, wozu sie teils vorgebohrt werden müssen. Zum Schluss die Holzkugel beschriften.
Page 143 top picture:
Botanicals: Chamaerops humilis, Olea europaea, Pinus pinea, Punica granatum, x Vuylstekeara Cultivar
Non-floral materials: *Wooden foot, wooden stick, wooden sphere, decorative star*
How to make it: *Drill a hole into the middle of the wooden foot, into which a wooden stick is stuck. Then, the botanicals and accessories are speared whereas some of them have to be predrilled. At the end, the wooden sphere is labelled.*

Seite 143 unten:
Werkstoffe: *Phalaenopsis Cultivar*
Materialien: Platte aus Granulat, Geweih, Kugel, Band
Wie wird's gemacht: Für dieses Wandbild wird das Geweih mit Draht auf einer Kunststoffgranulatplatte mit entsprechenden Bohrungen befestigt. Die durchsichtige Kugel wird mit Wasser gefüllt und an das Geweih gehängt.
Page 143 bottom picture:
Botanicals: Phalaenopsis Cultivar
Non-floral materials: *Board of granules, horns, ball, ribbon*
How to make it: *The horns for this mural are fixed onto an artificial board of granules with a wire and respective drills. The transparent ball is filled with water and suspended from the horns.*

Seite 144:
Werkstoffe: *Cornus alba 'Sibirica', Hippeastrum Cultivars, Olea europaea, Pinus mugo, Pinus pinea, Punica granatum*

Materialien: Gefäß, Zweigquader, Kugeln
Wie wird's gemacht: Der handelsübliche Zweigquader wird auf das Gefäß gelegt und dient als Steckhilfe für die Werkstoffe. Dabei gilt das Prinzip: Je mehr Blumen eingesteckt werden, desto mehr Halt hat der Quader.
Page 144:
Botanicals: Cornus alba 'Sibirica', Hippeastrum Cultivars, Olea europaea, Pinus mugo, Pinus pinea, Punica granatum
Non-floral materials: *Container, cuboid made of branches, spheres*
How to make it: *The usual cuboid is put onto a container and serves as an aid for arranging the plant materials. Thereby the following principle applies: The more flowers are inserted, the more hold is given to the cuboid.*

Seite 145:
Werkstoffe: *Hippeastrum vittatum, Leucadendron laureolum, Pinus mugo, Prunus spinosa, Scabiosa stellata,* Zimtrinde
Materialien: Gefäß, Dekostern
Wie wird's gemacht: Zuerst wird das Glasgefäß oben mit Kreppband beklebt. Anschließend die Zimtrinde mit Heißkleber befestigen und den Rand des Gefäßes mit *Leucadendron, Pinus, Prunus* und *Scabiosa* ausgestalten. Zum Schluss *Hippeastrum* einstellen.
Page 145:
Botanicals: Hippeastrum vittatum, Leucadendron laureolum, Pinus mugo, Prunus spinosa, Scabiosa stellata, *cinnamon bark*
Non-floral materials: *Container, decorative star*
How to make it: *First, the glass container is pasted with crepe tape on top. Then attach the cinnamon bark with hot glue and decorate the rim of the container with* Leucadendron, Pinus, Prunus *and* Scabiosa. *At the end, insert the* Hippeastrum.

Baum/*Tree*

Seite 148/149:
Werkstoffe: *Pinus nigra*
Materialien: Holzplatte, Metall, Bienenwachsplatte, Ständer, Dekosterne, Metallfolie, Kerzen, Kerzenhalter
Wie wird's gemacht: Für den Ständer wird eine quadratische Holzplatte gestrichen, und ein Rundmetall mit seitlichen Füßen als Einsteckhalterung für den Baum darauf geschraubt. Neben handelsüblichen Dekosternen werden zusätzlich solche aus Metallfolie und Bienenwachswaben gefertigt und in den Baum gehängt.
Page 148/149:
Botanicals: Pinus nigra
Non-floral materials: *Wooden board, metal, beeswax plate, stand, decorative stars, metal foil, candles, candlestick*
How to make it: *To construct the stand, a square wooden board is painted and a round metal stick with lateral feet is screwed as a fitting for the tree. Besides usual decorative stars additional stars of metal foil and beeswax combs are formed and suspended at the tree.*

Seite 150/151:
Werkstoffe: *Abies nordmanniana, Ilex aquifolium, Malus Cultivar, Pinus strobus*
Materialien: Lichterkette, Draht, Bänder, Kordeln, Holzsterne, Lebkuchen, Zuckerkränze, Birkenstammscheiben, Holzschmuck
Wie wird's gemacht: Die Tanne wird bis zur Hälfte im unteren Bereich von allen Zweigen befreit. Ein rundes Holzbrett rot streichen und den Stamm des Baumes mit der Platte verschrauben. An langen Bändern werden Kränze aus *Ilex*-Blättern und die anderen Dekoelemente befestigt und in den Baum gehangen. Die Lichterkette schmückt den oberen Bereich der Tanne.
Page 150/151:
Botanicals: Abies nordmanniana, Ilex aquifolium, Malus Cultivar, Pinus strobus
Non-floral materials: *Christmas lights, wire, ribbons, cords, wooden stars, ginger bread, sugar wreaths, birch bole discs, wooden decoration*
How to make it: *All the twigs are removed from the fir. Paint a round wooden board in red and screw the trunk of the tree with the board. Wreaths of* Ilex*-leaves and the other decorative elements are fixed onto long ribbons and suspended at the tree. The Christmas lights adorn the upper part of the fir.*

Seite 152/153:
Werkstoffe: *Cedrus atlantica 'Glauca', Helleborus niger, Lunaria annua*
Materialien: Gefäß, Lichterkette, Fiberglas, Pappe, Glasröhrchen, Dekosterne, Prismen, Kugeln, Spindeln, Eiszapfenanhänger
Wie wird's gemacht: Die Zeder wird in das Gefäß gepflanzt. Als zusätzliche Dekoelemente werden Sterne aus mit *Lunaria* beklebter Pappe und wellenförmige Elemente aus Fiberglasplatten geschnitten. Dann wird die Lichterkette im Baum angebracht und gebündelte *Lunaria*-Triebe werden hineingesteckt. Zum Schluss die Glasröhrchen mit den Christrosen und die restlichen Dekoelemente in den Baum hängen.
Page: 152/153:
Botanicals: Cedrus atlantica 'Glauca', Helleborus niger, Lunaria annua
Non-floral materials: *Container, Christmas lights, fibre glass, cardboard, glass tubes, decorative stars, prisms, balls, spindles, icicle pendant*
How to make it: *The cedar is planted in the container. Additional decorative elements are formed out of cardboard pasted with* Lunaria *and cut in the form of stars and undulating elements of fibre glass plates. Then, the tree is decorated with the Christmas lights and the bunch of* Lunaria*-shoots is inserted. At the end, hang the glass tubes containing the* Helleborus *and the rest of the decorative elements into the tree.*